Honest to Christ
Sir John Ford K.C.M.G., M.C.

A Challenge to the Bishops
of the Anglican Communion at their Conference
at Canterbury, Summer 1988

Any net income received by the author from the sale of HONEST TO CHRIST will be given to recognised charities, through the Charities Aid Foundation.

Honest to Christ

by

John Ford

1988
CHURCHMAN PUBLISHING LIMITED
WORTHING AND FOLKESTONE

© Copyright Sir John Ford 1988

Honest to Christ was first published in 1988 by
Churchman Publishing Limited
117 Broomfield Avenue
Worthing, West Sussex BN14 7SF

Publisher: E. Peter Smith

Represented in
Australia, Canada, New Zealand
and the United States of America

Distributed to the book trade by
Bailey Book Distribution Limited
Warner House, Wear Bay Road,
Folkestone, Kent CT19 6PH

All rights reserved worldwide

ISBN 1 85093 099 6

Typeset by Electronic Village of Richmond, Surrey
and printed in Great Britain by
Biddles Limited, of Guildford, Surrey

To my wife Emaline
who has had to put up with so much from me

The author gratefully acknowledges the help received from Caryl Horwood who so efficiently typed his manuscripts

Notice to readers of "Honest to Christ"

In this book the author challenges the Anglican Bishops to consider in July/August 1988 the issue at the end of their Conference of a Declaration of Belief and a Call to Action in the form of the draft proposed at the end of the book. If you agree with this, you are asked to complete Form B which appears at the end of the book and send it to your Diocesan Bishop.

The author has also suggested that Christian Support Groups should be formed and be provided with special material to help people imaginatively to meditate on the personality of Christ as **evidenced** by the New Testament reports of His life and sayings and by the people in whom He has most apparently dwelt down the centuries. The author is prepared to make available his own meditations on Christ as **evidenced** by His sayings as reported in the synoptic gospels and by the fourth gospel and is engaged on a further series of meditations on Christ as seen in Francis of Assisi. If you are interested in starting or joining a Support Group or in acquiring the author's meditations from which "Honest to Christ" was largely drawn, you are asked to complete Form A at the end of the book and to send it to him.

CONTENTS

		Page
	Foreword	11
	Part One	
Preamble:	Christ and Evolution	13
Chapter I	Christ, the Person on whom Evolution hinges	23
Chapter II	God, the Great First Cause	33
Chapter III	Evolution, God's mysterious process for the generation of personality at one with His	39
Chapter IV	The concept of Christ's mystical body as our Evolutionary doctrine	49
Chapter V	The problem of evil	57
Chapter VI	Heaven, hell, life and death	63

Chapter VII	Evolution and Atonement	69
Chapter VIII	The individual	73
Chapter IX	Vocation and the Priest	79
Chapter X	Prayer	83
Chapter XI	The future – Part Two	85

Part Two

Chapter XII	The Christian Clerical Establishments	89
Chapter XIII	The Role of the Clergy	95
Chapter XIV	The Adaptation of Christ's Mystical Body to Changing Circumstances	101
Chapter XV	1988: A Year of Crisis	109

Foreword

The first part of this book is a very personal reflection on the relationship between the historic Christ and Evolution. Starting from the hypothesis that Evolution, however it may ultimately be shown to work, is God's mysterious process for the generation of personality at one with His, I examine how far the observable facts square with the hypothesis. I conclude that the facts do indeed square with my assumption and that acceptance of it leads to the conclusion that Christ is the hinge on which the process turns; and that the development of Christ's mystical body over the past two millenia provides the best pointer to the future of God's creative design.

In his book "Honest to God" Bishop John Robinson sought to blow away concepts of God as a sort of super Father Christmas and to destroy the image of Him as a venerable white-haired patriarch. I have deliberately stolen from his title to call this book "Honest to Christ" because I believe that by setting Christ in His evolutionary context it reveals Him in a new light.

I also believe that acceptance of my hypothesis by the Christian churches would revolutionise their current thinking and practices and perhaps lead to advances in theology and ethics as sensational as those in science and technology which flowed directly and indirectly from Galileo and Newton.

Foreword

Having hitherto been unable to interest almost any clergy in even seriously considering my thesis let alone acting upon it, I have in part II attempted a challenge to the ecclesiastical establishment and metaphorically nailed my thesis to the door of Lambeth Palace. As one, like Luther acting under an inner compulsion, I have felt that I could not do otherwise. I ask therefore that all you among my readers who share my deep dissatisfaction with the current state of the Christian church establishments will grant me the indulgence of a sympathetic and understanding ear.

John Ford

Part I

Christ and Evolution

Preamble

In his book "The Sleepwalkers" Arthur Koestler describes how for centuries the accepted authority of Aristotle's thought held the human intellect in thrall. Because Aristotle had believed that the sun went round the earth the thinkers of Christendom believed the same, and their attempts to discover the secrets of the universe and to work out scientific explanations for its phenomena about them were all based on the hypothesis that Aristotle was right; and so they ultimately got nowhere. Only when Galileo proved that Aristotle was wrong and that the earth did in fact go round the sun did people stop wasting their time pursuing a dead end and resume doing what wise men before Aristotle had been doing – pursuing the facts of life. The results have been sensational. Scientific knowledge has taken a leap forward, and the way has been opened for the technological revolution of our age.

In its way the publication of Darwin's "Origin of the Species" was just as liberating an event. Since the foundation of Christendom some two thousand years ago – and before that, since the ancient Jewish traditions

Preamble

about the creation had been accepted centuries before under circumstances now lost to our knowledge in the mists of time – people had interpreted their belief in man's creation by God as an event comparable to an artist's creation of a new work of art, and their philosophy was based on a more or less literal acceptance of the Genesis story.

The publication of Galileo's discovery was naturally unwelcome to the "establishment" of his day. To begin with it undermined the credibility of the existing scientific authorities and threatened the position of all those people who were enjoying a respectability, status and standard of living based on that credibility; even worse it threatened also religious authority, because the Church's leaders had also accepted Aristotle; and, because of the interdependence of the church and state, it could also be seen as a potential threat to secular rulers: if such a basic doctrine as the sun's circulation of the earth could successfully be challenged, where would the new attitude of enquiry stop? The Inquisition was called in, and Galileo was forced publicly to recant. But the force of his discovery was so great that no one could in fact leash again the new thinking that he had unleashed. The observable facts were too important and too obvious to be ignored. Moreover the church leaders could draw comfort from the fact that Galileo's scientific discoveries did not directly challenge the prerogatives of the Christian church: the mysteries of religion and the explained facts of science were distinct,

Preamble

and the fields of astronomy and physics were not concerned with Christian theology or ethics; and these were the subjects of their expertise and the foundation of their position and status.

The publication of Darwin's theory of Evolution was even more unwelcome to the religious establishment of Christendom, since it challenged – or seemed to challenge – the very fundamentals of their faith. The accuracy of the Bible was openly put in question, and such accepted doctrines as the creation of man in God's image, the origin and nature of sin, and the atoning sacrifice of Jesus of Nazareth on the cross were directly queried. But the Christian church leaders, even if they had so wished, could not have suppressed Darwin as they tried to suppress Galileo: by the end of the nineteenth century Church and State had largely become separate and distinct while the forces of secular materialism were rapidly growing and, boosted in particular by the revolutionary ideas of Marx, were already threatening the Church and attracting away an increasing mass of the population; moreover the Christian leaders were further weakened by their own disunity. The very fact that Christendom was divided among rival Christian sects weakened authority; and even the Church of Rome was unable to pontificate with the effect which it had had in prereformation times when it was virtually the sole religious authority in the civilisation of the West. As the twentieth century wore on it became increasingly

Preamble

apparent how unsatisfactory the reaction of the church leaders had been.

On the one hand the authorities of the Church of Rome closed ranks, reinforced papal authority with the doctrine of papal infallibility and seemingly tried to carry on as if Darwin had never existed. On the other hand Christian fundamentalists, who based their faith on a literal interpretation of the Bible, rejected Darwinian Evolution and sought as far as lay within their power to suppress its teaching. In between, perhaps a majority of committed priests and laymen, tried to avoid too much thought about the implications and to concentrate on the traditional message of God's love through Christ.

I grew up in the interwar years in a European society whose foundation was largely shattered by the Great War of 1914–18 and threatened by the second even worse upheaval of 1939–45. I was fortunate in having loving Christian parents who were active members of that committed majority in the middle of the Christian spectrum. From them I caught a simple faith and personal acquaintance with Christ for which no words of gratitude are adequate. But, as I grew older and more experienced, I became increasingly worried by Christians' attitudes towards modern concepts of Evolution and the development of human behaviour. It seemed to me that if there is a God – and I believe there is – He must be Truth; and that if Christ is indeed alive and His personality is capable of absorbing and being absorbed

Preamble

by individuals – as I believe – He must enable people to interpret phenomena in such a way as to lead them to a greater perception of the truth.

For longer than I can remember I have taken the leaflets of the Bible Reading Fellowship and most days read them and the appointed passage of the Bible. By the time I was thirty I felt increasingly dissatisfied with this exercise. Spurred on by William Temple's "Readings in St John's Gospel", I worked slowly through that gospel meditating on each passage and ending each meditation with a prayer. I decided at the outset that I would regard the person of Christ as the yardstick on which I would base my measurements and the litmus against which I would test my interpretations; and that if I came across some passage which seemed to conflict with observable facts which I could not rationally deny then I would prayerfully put it on one side without rejecting it and in the hope that in time I would perceive the truth in spite of my own fallibility on all counts. After many years and much revision of those meditations I started a similar exercise based on the sayings of Christ as reported in the synoptic gospels; and the two exercises covered more than thirty years.

During that period I became acquainted with the writing of Teilhard de Chardin, the Jesuit palaeontologist whose book "The Phenomenon of Man" sought to marry the theology of the Church of Rome with the concepts of Evolution. The power of his thought, in so far as I can

Preamble

understand the complexity of his language and thought processes, has been a spur to my own thinking and my conviction that Christian theology must face up to Evolution. I owe him much more than I can say and believe that in time he will be given the credit which is his due. Thanks largely to him, I have felt myself drawn into the conviction that there is an Evolutionary explanation of the phenomenon of Christ and that until that explanation is accepted and understood the people of Christendom will be "sleepwalking" in the same way as people were sleepwalking in the fields of astronomy and physics until Galileo woke them up. I suspect that it is partly because we are sleepwalking that Christendom is apparently losing its appeal to the educated and most rapidly gaining adherents among the uneducated, particularly in Africa and Latin America.

In science it is often an accepted method of procedure to imagine an hypothesis and then see whether the observable facts fit it. When they do, the assumption is that the hypothesis is true. If later new facts suggest that the original hypothesis was incorrect, it is either discarded or amended as necessary to fit the facts. The basic facts do not change; what changes is the human understanding of them.

Observable aspects of the human intelligence are its fallibility and its limitations. It is bound by the dimensions of height, length, breadth and time which seem to bind the human race on earth, and it is capable of seeing things

Preamble

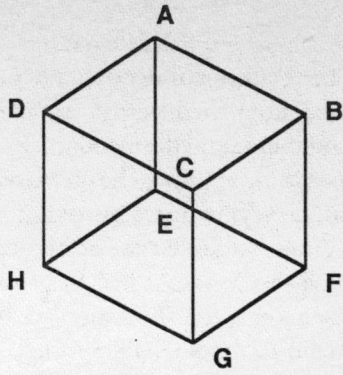

in two or more ways. For example if I look at the bare outline of a cube thus I cannot tell how that cube lies. At one moment it may look as if the corner C is nearest to me, at another corner E. Other examples of this phenomenon can be adduced, and it applies in different ways to my perceptions, e g when someone does something which causes me to see him in a new light which changes my perception of him. I have felt that a proper humility demands that I bear this very much in mind in my approaches to the Truth.

In trying through prayer and meditation to approach more nearly to the unchanging Truth I have accepted as my hypothesis that the process of Evolution (however it may ultimately be shown to work) is God's mysterious process for the generation of human personality at one with His. Against this I have tested the historic evidence of the person of Christ and of the scriptures as set out

Preamble

in the canonical books of the Bible. I have also tried to bear in mind the traditional doctrines of Christendom, in so far as I, an untrained person and no theologian, have understood them, and the evidence of some of those in whom Christ has dwelt down the past twenty centuries since his crucifixion; but I recognise that this evidence is so vast and unfathomable that no individual can do more than touch the fringe of it.

In the following chapters I start off with the historic fact of Christ who to me seems the hinge on which the whole evolutionary process turns; I next reflect on the person and nature of God whom Christ revealed; and then finally consider the problem of evil and the relationship between God and man and its implications for human conduct. Finally I set out a vision of the future and some personal conclusions. I do not put forward the following chapters as anything more than the product of one ordinary and fallible human mind. I put them forward personally since I believe that they are only of value in so far as they are genuinely held ideas based on experience and not on theory. I hope that by helping to stimulate more thought on the implications of Evolution they will help deepen insight into the wonderful ways of God. The more I know, the more I know I need to know. My attempts to enter into the mystery of God have not for me lessened that mystery. The more I see it the more wonderful it appears. The satisfaction which I have derived from my years of meditation is the satisfaction not of knowledge but of awe and love. And, after all, what greater satisfaction could anyone reasonably demand than that!

CHAPTER I

Christ, the Person on whom Evolution hinges

The person of Jesus of Nazareth is a fact of history just as are the persons whose existence is attested in written records, whether notorious as great figures of history such as Alexander the Great or unknown people of whom the only memory now lies in some birth certificate in the public records. There is no doubt that someone called Jesus did live about two thousand years ago, was executed and was the founder of Christianity.

My main external source of knowledge about Him is contained in the four gospels of the New Testament. Tradition attributes two of them to Matthew and John, two of Jesus's inner circle of twelve chosen followers and friends, and the other two to a man called Mark, who may have been the boy who fled from the Garden of Gethsemane at the time of Jesus's arrest, and to a doctor called Luke, who was recorded as one of the earliest Christian missionaries and who also wrote the Acts, a history of the early years of the Christian church. Vast effort has been expended by scholars down the ages in

Honest to Christ

studying the texts of books of the New Testament; their consensus appears to be that they are genuine, that the so-called synoptic gospels of Matthew, Mark and Luke draw on some other now lost source of personal knowledge of Jesus, perhaps Peter's personal accounts, and that all were probably written within the lifetime of some who had personally known Jesus. In the absence of evidence to the contrary, I thus find it reasonable to assume that within the limitations of the writers and their earliest copyists the gospels are historic documents and do reveal Truth about Christ.

Two other facts seem to me to lend them veracity. The first is the apparent motives of the writers. Each obviously writes under the personal conviction that Jesus was what He claimed to be, that He did in fact rise from the grave and that He remains alive and active as He said He would be. The writers obviously believe the message that they are recording, and they have no visible motive for writing as they did save a desire to put over the truth as they saw it. The writing of their records was a danger to them because of the persecution of the early Church, their personal integrity shines through their writing and is supported by the traditional views of early Christian writers, and they had no obvious motive for deliberately trying to deceive.

In his book "Who Moved the Stone?" Frank Morison examined the facts and came to the conclusion that the story of the resurrection was true. The truth of facts of ancient history seems virtually impossible to prove, and I am certainly not equipped to argue against the four Evangelists, Frank Morison or those who accept the truth of the Resurrection. I do, however, know enough about human nature and the way in which people now think and did in Roman times think, to know that the Resurrection story was strange and unbelievable. That a scattered band of largely uneducated and dispirited followers of a criminal executed in one of the cruellest and most degrading manners possible suddenly regrouped, became charged with a sincere conviction, overcame the scepticism of Greek and Roman thought and laid the foundations for a movement that has changed the face of history is a fact of history; and it is a fact which argues powerfully in favour of acceptance of the Christian belief in the Resurrection of Jesus of Nazareth as recorded in the gospels. Gamaliel had a point when he argued (Acts V 38–39) that the Apostles should be left alone because "if this counsel or this work be of men, it will come to nought: but if it be of God you cannot overthrow it; lest haply you be found to fight against God"; and Saint Paul put the matter succinctly when he wrote "If Christ has not been raised, then our preaching is empty and your faith without foundation". (1 Cor XV 14). The evidence clearly points to the fact that something very remarkable did happen after Jesus was buried, and that leads me to Jesus's claim to be God.

This claim seems to me to be both implicitly and

explicitly recorded in all four gospels. The fact that the gospels suggest that Jesus's awareness of His relationship with God was a developing one as He grew up and acquired knowledge and experience, gives added credibility to the belief that He was both God and man, and as man subject in His humanity to the limits of humanity. The claim was blasphemous according to the standards of the society in which He lived; it was for this blasphemy that the Sanhedrin condemned Him, and the scandal of it must greatly have worried His closest friends and followers. Yet they accepted it and recorded it and recorded also that they did not understand Him until after His resurrection and the coming of the Holy Spirit to inspire them.

I see ample evidence in the gospels that Jesus was most careful about the use of language: for example, He was most cautious about allowing His followers to describe Him as the promised Messiah because people had preconceived ideas about what sort of person the Messiah would be, and to use that term about himself would be to set Himself within those preconceived ideas. When he is reported to have said to some of His Jewish antagonists: "I tell you most solemnly, before Abraham ever was, I AM", (John VIII 58), He was appropriating the ancient Jewish name for God to Himself. They knew He was and tried to stone Him. John, perhaps the best educated and most intelligent of the twelve apostles, knew he was, and, whatever he thought at the time, ultimately recognised the truth of the claim. An ordinary person such as myself has not the time, nor the energy nor the intellect to analyse all the evidence for or against; but if I decide one way or the other my decision must fit into my overall philosophy and my perception of the circumstances under which I find myself. A decision against the record of the Evangelists and the traditions of Christendom would seem to conflict with all my perceptions and the unity which makes of them a cohesive whole. A decision for the record requires the act of faith to believe in God and the miraculous. But before I deal with that, there are two other aspects of the phenomenon of Jesus which seem to me essential to consider in the context of my original hypothesis.

If Evolution is God's mysterious process for the generation of personality at one with His and it moves forward on a time scale, I would expect progress in the process. Is progress visible in the process of harmonisation of human personality with the personality of God? I suggest that the evidence undoubtedly shows that it is; and that the Advent of Jesus is consistent with that progress and that what has gone on after is consistent too. Just as progress before His coming turned on Him, so progress afterwards has continued to turn on Him.

A day is an appreciable time in my life, eternity for a microbe that lives just hours, and only a trice in the context of Evolution or even the history of the human species. We have no knowledge of when or how the first person appeared, who in his ability to ponder and reflect was distinct from the mammals and all other creatures who had preceded him. The evidence suggests that the first human beings were far more limited than we in many of their capabilities. Their struggle for survival in a hostile environment without any but the simplest means of coping with their bare existence, their race's lack of collective knowledge and means of communication and their individual ignorance deprived them of material and intellectual resources which have become taken for granted by later generations. Theirs was the first glimmering of human intelligence; theirs the budding of the human spirit. In their dark ages of the human past who knows what concepts of God first came to be held or what rites of worship first expressed man's awe. Ancestor worship, the circumstances of human society such as it was and other influences now unknown must all have played their part in the formation of peoples' concept of God and their relation to Him. With no means of communication between scattered groups of people, it was natural that beliefs and practices were diverse and that what was common to them was attributable to the common thread of human nature linking them. Monotheism, it seems, developed slowly after countless centuries; and in one nation, the Jewish, it lastingly took root and flourished. There it developed as the Jewish society developed; and the Jews' perception of their God, their relationship to Him and the regulation of that relationship with Him reflected the changes in their circumstances and their thinking. Abraham (only to begin with) probably thought of God in terms of a divine tyrant demanding human sacrifice; the God of vengeance of Samuel's perception seems far removed from the God about whom Hosea and Isaiah spoke. Yet Abraham, Samuel, Hosea, Isaiah and Jesus all worshipped the same unchanging God. What changed and developed was perceptions of God; and looking at the Old Testament I see running through it a thread of progress which culminates in Jesus, the promised Messiah of Jews and the Christ of Christendom.

There are, however, two ways of looking at the Old Testament record, and some people prefer to take it literally and to regard it as direct revelation by God Himself: where the prophet prophecies the prophecy is to be taken as the literal word of God; and where the writer describes what happened his description is to be accepted as literally accurate, even though the Old Testament is full of poetry and the art of the poet is to convey a message through imagery and music and magic of words. If Jesus could not use the term Messiah about Himself because, as commonly understood, it would have conveyed the wrong ideas to His listeners, then it is hardly likely that God would have from the first appearance of the human species expected people to have been capable of accepting any full revelation of Himself. Had He done so, it would have been logical for Him at the outset to send into the world his Word made flesh.

The more I see the Old Testament in the context of the New, the more it seems to me to be read as the record of the Jews' developing perception of God and of the setting of the stage when it would be possible for God to reveal Himself in the highest terms capable of being understood by human beings – the terms of a human life perfectly lived on earth by His Son. In the setting of the stage timing seems important; and the timing of Christ's advent does seem to coincide with a point on the evolutionary scale where elements in the society of Palestine were receptive enough and the communications within the Roman Empire good enough to ensure the disseminations of the Good News which Jesus created.

But if the coming of Christ is to be seen as evolutionary, as a stage in a progression, progress after His death and resurrection must also be visible. Indeed it is. In John's account of Jesus's prayer on the night of His arrest (John XVII 20–23) he quotes Jesus as praying thus:

> "I pray not only for these but for those who through their words will believe in me. May they all be one. Father may they be one in us, as you are in me and I am in You…With me in them and You in me may they be so completely one…;"

and it is clear that John envisaged that, with the help of the Holy Spirit, Jesus would in some mystical way both absorb and be absorbed by future generations of believers.

Christ, the Person on whom Evolution hinges

This doctrine of the mystical body of Christ needs to be examined in more detail later; it suggests that Christ's mystical body must be developing as its human members develop and thus seems wholly compatible with an acceptance of Christ in an evolutionary context.

I conclude therefore that my understanding of Christ is compatible with my original hypothesis about Evolution: that it is based on historic facts and is reasonable; but that it does require an act of faith about the truth of the gospel. The taking of that act of faith automatically includes an act of faith in belief in the existence of God for which the main evidence lies in Christ. How does the evolutionary picture square with the Christian concept of God? That logically must be examined next.

CHAPTER II
God, the Great First Cause

Voltaire, the famous French sceptic of the eighteenth century, wrote two pungent truths" "Dieu defini est dieu fini" (God defined is God finished) and "Si Dieu n'avait pas existé, l'homme l'aurait invente" (If God had not existed, man would have invented Him). Both sentences are tantalising because, like the bare outline of the cube, they can be regarded in two ways and appear true in each. To the atheist the first clinches the argument that God does not exist, and the second provides good reason for explaining why people have created a non-existent God in their imagination. To the theist it is evident that no creature can be as capable as its creator or fully capable of understanding Him; the theist also sees that man, God's creature, needs some belief about his origins and needs it so much, if he is to have any logical philosophy, that he would indeed have invented God had God not been there; and that in his groping towards an understanding of God man does tend to invent a God of his own imagination rather than accept the God Who is. The dying Inca who wrote that ancient prayer which can be translated thus spoke for everyone who like Pascal has gazed into the heavens and been overcome with awe:

>"O Uira-cocha, Lord of All, First Cause,
>If thou art male in thy life-giving force
>Or female in they wondrous procreation,
>O all creation's Lord, if thou art both,
>Oh, tell me where thou art great Lord Supreme!
>Thy throne or sceptre is't perhaps around?
>And thou? Perhaps below perhaps above
>Thou dwell'st? O tell me now! O, hear my prayer!
>And be thy dwelling in the sky above
>Or be it in the darkling sea beneath,
>Where e'er it be, now hearken to my cry,
>O Lord of Lords, Creator of all men!
>O Master mine, my eyes do fail me now
>In this my longing for a sight of thee,
>And all my powers of thought do fail indeed
>In this my one my sole desire to know.
>Oh, that I might see thee, know thee, feel thee,
>Gaze at thee and comprehend thy being!
>Oh look on me, for thou – thou knowest me.
>The sun – the moon – the stars – the day – the night
>The spring and winter too – O Uira Coch' –
>All these are not ordained in vain by thee;
>They travel all at thy behest, O Lord;
>And all arrive at thy predestined ends.

God, the Great First Cause

Thou reignest over all the Universe.
Oh, hear me now! Oh, favour me,
And do not, do not let it be
That I should tire, that I should die!''

Down the ages there have been plenty of people ruthless and arrogant enough to try to invent a god to satisfy other people's longings and to suit their own interests.

Faced with the hypothesis that God exists, I have only three choices of attitude to adopt. The first is to deny the hypothesis and adopt the atheist line that God does not exist. The second is neither to deny nor accept the hypothesis but to argue that the answer lies outside the realm of human comprehension, that it does not matter anyhow, and that there is therefore no point in pursuing the matter. The third is to accept the hypothesis and act accordingly.

My problem with atheism stems from the fact that it is unproveable. The time-bound human intellect can no more prove that God does not exist than it can prove that God does exist. Because I cannot prove the truth of atheism I have to see whether such a theory squares with my observation of the world about me. If there is no Great First Cause, whence the start of things? If there is no truth, whence logic and the power of rational thought? If there is no purpose, whence progress? Clearly, if there is no God, my hypothesis that Evolution is God's mysterious process for the generation of personality at one with His is nonsense. But so too is Evolution; and its whole process has to be attributed to random selection and pure chance, a concept which is obvious non-sense, since a sense of logic plays no part in it and is denied by it. A rejection of God thus seems rationally untenable, and impossible to square with my consciousness of time and of the world about me; moreover it in no way satisfies my desire to run my life according to some comprehensive and rational philosophy, nor does it meet that mysterious longing which I sense within me and which seems to lie outside the realms of the material. I marvel at the beauty of creation and I am filled with awe when contemplating the majesty of the Universe. Is that awe but the product of an empty imagination and deceitful senses? In the depth of my being I sense that that cannot be.

The second agnostic attitude is more beguiling. It neatly avoids the necessity for proofs and acts of faith about the unproveable; and it provides the lazy with a reason for not wasting time on the allegedly unknowable. It does not have to square with any philosophy, because it regards as intellectually fruitless the pursuit of any key to a philosophy; and it leaves the holder free to pursue any line of intellectual enquiry he may wish without encumbering himself with any hypotheses he cannot prove. My trouble with agnosticism is that it does not satisfy my innermost longing for some wholeness of which I and all observable creation are a part. It is not compatible with my hypothesis about Evolution and would not be compatible with any other hypothesis. It

God, the Great First Cause

does not square with my knowledge of Christ, and it explains nothing. It accepts that a hypothetical approach can be of value in scientific research but rejects that approach when it comes to philosophical and religious enquiry.

Thus I seem faced willy nilly with accepting the hypothesis that God indeed exists. It fits my hypothesis about Evolution. It fits my knowledge of Christ. It satisfies my need of a comprehensive philosophy and my seeming emotional needs; and it seems to do the same for other people, particularly those I most admire.

But I am deeply conscious that there is a difference between accepting that hypothesis willy nilly, as I would accept Einstein's proposition that space is curved (the proposition is meaningless to me: I have neither the knowledge nor brains to dispute it, and my and others' knowledge of Einstein leads me to accept it on faith because Einstein's reasoning has been shown to be trusted with good cause), and accepting it as something which has the full weight of my will and conviction based on real experience. My acceptance of the fact that very hot iron burns, is of a different order to my acceptance of Einstein's theories. I recognize that my acceptance of the truth that God exists must depend on more than just an act of faith and reason.

And that is where I am thrown back again to Christ. Even His closest friends could not understand and accept His revelation of God until He had died, risen, sent the

Holy Spirit and begun to live in them as He lived in the Father. It seems logical – and in accord with Christian doctrine – to assume that what was true of them must also be true of me; and my observation of the history of Christianity leads me to believe that there have been many Christians who have accepted the faith passively and at bottom only nominally and far fewer who have made it an integral part of their being through their total commitment to Christ and the way in which they have become an integral part of His mystical body. The more I contemplate the latter the more deeply do I sense that God exists and that He is indeed the Person, the Love and the Truth, whom Christ reveals.

Having accepted that God exists and has been revealed by Christ it now seems logical to examine the phenomenon of Evolution to see whether it is compatible with the concept that it is indeed God's mysterious process.

CHAPTER III

Evolution, God's mysterious process for the generation of personality at one with His

The truth of Evolution, like the truths of events of recorded history, does not appear to be proveable in the sense that the truth of a mathematical equation can be proved; moreover there are such gaps in our knowledge that any theory of Evolution based on the facts as revealed in the world about us merely points to some such process of development rather than clearly defining it. There does seem to be a graduation of matter from the simplest elements to the most complicated, and it does look as if the simpler forms of things preceded the more complicated. The earliest rock strata, eg those of the moon, have not yielded fossil evidence of life in even the simplest form. Evidence of the existence of the simplest living organisms precedes that of the more complicated. Unicellular species seem to have preceded the multicellular, plants to have come before animals, insects and reptiles before mammals and less cerebral mammals before the human species. There are great gaps in human knowledge of the development of the human species, but what we do know about the earliest specimens of homo erectus suggests that he was less cerebral than I and lived a much simpler form of existence, more akin than mine to the existence, for example, of the apes. Studies of human behaviour suggest that there are considerable parallels between human behaviour, eg over sexual courting, and some animals' behaviour.

By and large the clergy seem to have avoided discussion of this phenomenon. Probably because one of his greatest interests was palaeontology, Teilhard de Chardin wrestled with the problem and tried to fit it into the theology of the Christian church of Rome. As a Jesuit he had submitted himself to the discipline of that church and he chose to remain subject to that discipline. Throughout his lifetime his theories were the subject of great suspicion among the church authorities, and since his death and the publication of his writings the Christian establishment has handled them with extreme caution and so far as possible tried to keep them in the lowest profile. In that they have been aided by the complicated nature of Teilhard's thinking.

Darwin's first concept of Evolution has undergone modifications as more evidence has come to light, and I do not have the specialised knowledge or intention to write a critique of Evolution. The consensus of scientists

Evolution, God's mysterious process

seems to be that there is such a process and that it probably develops in stages by mutation, development under environmental conditions and survival through adaptation to the environment. Thus higher forms of living things come to the top because they survive best. While this consensus produces a coherent account of the pattern and manner of development, it does not explain the rationality of it. Indeed those who argue that mutations and survival are often determined by chance see no rational purpose, beginning or end to the process.

Noticing how a solution of certain chemicals suddenly reacted and produced crystals once the solution had reached a certain strength, Teilhard saw a parallel with the way in which he thought evolution might have progressed, and put forward a hypothetic law of complexity consciousness to explain it. He saw in evolution the earliest phenomena being the simplest and the least conscious and the last, the human species, being the most complicated and the most conscious. He saw the pattern of progress being one in which atoms developed from the simplest to the most complicated until a time of sudden change occurred and molecules appeared; molecules did the same until suddenly viruses and cells appeared; they in their turn became more complicated bacteria and ultimately all the species of living things. In their development too Teilhard saw the same process at work as the struggle for survival weeded out and the pressures of numbers (like the strength of the chemical solution) forced change. In mammals he saw in their development the growing complexity of their nervous system; and in the development of man he saw the development of a new phenomenon "person", as distinct from what had preceded it as the molecule had been from the atom. In his vision of this process Teilhard saw two forces at work. The first he called external or tangential energy, the energy created by the pressure of things rubbing up against each other. The second he called internal or radial energy, the energy created by the divine force within to be sensed for example in concepts of consciousness, intelligence, mind, psyche, soul, spirit and God, which he saw as the forward impetus of a process starting with its alpha (beginning) in God and ending with its omega (end) also in God.

As (I hope) a rational being I find that I can look at the individual stages of Evolution and see them in two ways: I can see them as the results of chance and the survival of the fittest, or I can see them as the result of some rational law of creation. But when I survey the wonders of creation and of the phenomenon of man as a whole my mind cannot conceive that all that could be the product of blind chance. Some statisticians may argue that a team of monkeys playing at random over the keyboards of numerous typewriters might in the end type out the works of Shakespeare, but to my mind that is too far-fetched to be credible; moreover there are apparently laws of probability. Lastly, if I accept the hypothesis about

Evolution, God's mysterious process

the determining causes being chance and survival, that is incompatible with reason and with all my knowledge of Christ and God.

On the other hand some concept of Evolution similar to or based on Teilhard's theory does seem compatible with a concept of God. Is it equally compatible with God as revealed by Christ?

The historic Christ was man, Christians believe, as well as God. As man He voluntarily accepted the limitations of the man of His day and age. The Jew of the Roman Empire at the time of Tiberius was the creature of his country at those times. His education was limited to the education of the society in which he lived, and His knowledge of the material world about Him was limited to the knowledge of His day. If Jesus was wholly man, His knowledge would have been similar to other people's. If they thought the earth was flat, He would have done so. If they had thought, which they didn't, that epilepsy was an illness brought about by the malfunctioning of a gland in the human body, He would probably have thought so too; and the vast book of modern technology would have been as closed to Him as it was to the other people of His era. We have no record that Jesus ever attempted to expound on the scientific theories of His day or to lead the people of His day into the fields of later technology. In the absence of evidence we must assume that He did not. There is, however, ample evidence that He accepted the Jews' traditional beliefs about God, that

He was steeped in and accepted the Jewish law and the prophets; and there is some evidence that He may have been influenced by the most up-to-date thinking of Jewish sects such as the Essenes. It is clear that Jesus accepted the essential message of Genesis that man was created by God in the image of God, and that in arguing His case with the Jewish establishment He was adept at quoting the scriptures to prove His point. It is also clear from the gospel accounts that in His stories and metaphors and similes He often exaggerated to make a point, using both humour and scorn when necessary. His vision of God was built on the vision of the Jewish prophets who had preceded Him, clouded though their vision had been because of their imperfections. Moreover, if we look at those prophets' vision of God, we do see some progression towards Christ's revelation. What Isaiah saw is more akin to that revelation than what Abraham or Isaac saw; what Hosea saw nearer to the truth than Samuel. Yet there is all the difference between their vision and Christ's personally authoritative revelation!

The concept of Christ's mystical body is so important that I must devote a separate chapter to it. Suffice to say here that if Christ, as Christians believe, does live on in the world in the people who have absorbed Him and been absorbed by Him then it is logical that His human outlook develops as the human mind, experience and knowledge develop, and that there can be nothing static about the human race's relationship with God or its vision of God.

The harsh fact of Evolution's struggle of the fittest for survival seems at first sight hard to square with the hypothesis that Evolution is the process of the God of Love revealed by Jesus; and consideration of that falls rather to a separate chapter on the problem of good and evil which logically would seem to follow my next on the mystical body of Christ.

The central fact about Evolution does, however, seem clear. Whatever the process and the reason or unreason behind it, it has produced a new phenomenon – the person.

In one sense it may be argued that the expression of the human personality is what all art is about. The German novelist Kleist was almost obsessed with the unaccountability of the human personality and wrote of it as this riddle of a thing that we possess that comes from we know not where and leads us we know not where. Teilhard seems to me right to regard personality as a new phenomenon, something that exists as any other phenomenon of the material world about me exists and yet different in having no height, length, breadth or weight and being in some sense outside the limits of time and space; nor is it really definable just as God cannot be defined. I cannot grasp a personality as I can understand, say, an internal combustion engine; nor can I break it down into components for analysis; like a joke or a symphony, what it really is and the effect which it has upon me disappear in the process of such analysis.

To gain insight into personality I need to love people and absorb the artists' insights; and these, whether they be conveyed through the media of music or of language or of the visual arts, are conveyed at least as much, if not more, through the imagination and emotions as through dry reasoning.

The psalms and many of the books of the Old Testament are shot through with poetry and need to be read and understood as such. Modern research and archaeology have done much to validate the Old Testament as history; but to treat it all as a literal account of historic events would seem as unrealistic and as deceiving as to consider Jesus's parables as accounts of actual people and events; yet both in their totality can be regarded as pointers to the Truth. I see nothing in Teilhard's interpretation of Evolution to conflict with the concept in Genesis that God created man in His own image. It may be argued that there is a conflict with the Genesis doctrine of the Fall and with the Christian doctrines of heaven and hell and the Atonement; but that deserves a later chapter to itself.

That God is a mystery stems of necessity from my concept of Him; and it is therefore both natural and intellectually acceptable that His processes of operation should be a mystery veiled from my limited understanding. That His mysterious process of Evolution has created personality seems evident from the facts in so far as I and others know them. What of the evidence to support the last part of my hypothesis that the purpose of Evolution is to generate personality at one with the Creator's. Here the evidence is Christ and what He revealed about God and taught about heaven and hell and life and the entering into a state of oneness with God. As later chapters will show I believe that what Christ taught on these subjects in no way invalidates my hypothesis about Evolution: on the contrary it seems to support it and make an acceptance of the fact of Evolution all the more essential to a coherent Christian philosophy. In the meantime I hope that the reasoning in this chapter has been adequate to show that an acceptance of my hypothesis about Evolution is neither incompatible with the facts of Evolution nor with the historic Christ's revelation of God.

CHAPTER IV

The concept of Christ's mystical body as an Evolutionary doctrine

In his study of mysticism "The Perennial Philosophy" Aldous Huxley drew convincingly together the evidence about the ability of certain individuals to achieve some form of unitary knowledge about the Ground of their Being. He showed how to do so they had had to become loving, pure in heart and pure in spirit, and he recognised the impossibility of any unloving and impure person's being able to understand what they had experienced: individuals cannot grasp or convey mystical knowledge through the operation of the reason, only by adopting the life-style of the loving and the pure. Huxley therefore went straight to the "saints" of history for his evidence and saw little point in consulting professional historians or theologians. As an agnostic he saw a common thread running through the experience of the great mystics of the world's major religions; but, because he had not accepted Jesus, he equated Jesus with the other mystics. In that fact I who have accepted the historic Christ see the flaw in Huxley's study; but that flaw does not disprove the evidence nor invalidate much of Huxley's conclusion. According to the four evangelists Jesus was quite clear about His unitary knowledge of God:

> "I know where I came from and where I am going..."
>
> "I am not alone, the one who sent me is with me..."
>
> "If you knew me you would know my Father as well..."
>
> "I do nothing of myself; what the Father has taught me is what I preach..."
>
> "I know my own as my own know me, just as the Father knows me and I know the Father..."
>
> "The Father and I are one..."
>
> "The father is in me and I am in the Father..."
>
> "You must believe me when I say that I am in the Father and the Father is in me..."

It is also evident that Jesus's followers were until His crucifixion and resurrection quite unable to grasp what He was getting at. Only after the mystical experience of Pentecost when they had been touched with the power of the Holy Spirit were they on track to an understanding. Even then it was years later after much suffering, prayer and mediation when John finally distilled his written account of the Good News.

It took more time before believers really began to

glimpse a vision of the mystical body of Christ; and the Christian saints through the power of love and the purity of their living have achieved a clarity of vision which is outside the grasp of lesser mortals. Like Aldous Huxley I can go to the Christian saints for valid evidence and, unlike him, do so in the faith that the Truth does in fact lie in Christ.

Over two thousand years the evidence of the saints is comprehensive – so vast in quantity and so shrouded in the mists of time that no one person could begin to comprehend it. As an unregenerate, fallible and ordinary person tarred by and stuck to the material world about me with all its imperfections, all I can do it to touch the fringe of the evidence and to accept what I can of the evidence of those particular saints whose appeal is greatest to me:

Saint Paul who rings in my ears with his triumphant "I live, yet not I; but Christ lives in me".

Saint Francis, the little Poor Man, who devoted himself to poverty and to being as much like His Master as possible, dances before my eyes; and, whether or not it was actually his, this prayer attributed to him is as much mine as my imperfections will allow, "Dear Master, grant me two graces before I die, the first that I may feel in my body all the pain and grief which You felt in Your Passion; the second that I may feel in my soul that exceeding great love which drove You to suffer so willingly to save sinners".

Theresa of Lisieux whose aim was to be so full of love that she did everything out of love of Christ.

Theresa of Avila who wrote "Christ has no body now on earth but yours; no hands but yours; no feet but yours; yours are the eyes through which are to look out Christ's compassion to the world; yours are the feet with which He is to go about doing good; yours are the hands with which He is to bless people now". (It would not have been inconsistent had she added "yours is the brain with which He is to go on thinking; yours the soul in which He is to live.")

If what Paul said was true of the Christian saint in his time, I see no reason to doubt why it should be true now. And it is that participation in the living Christ which differentiates the Christian mystic from the non-Christian. Buddha and the mystics of the Far East were children of a largely Hindu world who believed in a cyclical concept of time where all creatures went round and round some vast cone of life which all souls were doomed to circulate either at the bottom in the bodies of the lowest creatures or up the scale in those of the higher. Their only hope of escape from this painful process was to slip into the Nirvana of nothingness through the hole at the top of the cone. There seems nothing compatible with Evolution in that philosophy; yet the development of that philosophy is compatible with a development prior to the advent of Christ of the power of individuals to attain to a unitary knowledge of God.

The concept of Christ's mystical body as an Evolutionary doctrine

I suggest that in that context the evidence of the non-Christian mystics is valid.

I have recognised from the outset that, time-bound as I am, I cannot ever hope to understand the timeless or to perceive the time-bound in the context of the timeless. Even if the personality seems to me to some extent unbound by the limits of time and space, I still have to reflect about it in a time- and space-bound frame of thought. If I look now at the mystical body of Christ and look back to what existed before His incarnation, I see that His incarnation brought about a radical change in human circumstances. Before the personality of God was not present in the world in the way it was afterwards. Before people were groping towards an understanding because they had been given no complete revelation; and the evidence can be interpreted to suggest that they had not been given a complete revelation because they were not ready for it. Afterwards they had been given the revelation in the highest and most complete terms which the human mind is capable of understanding. Afterwards there was a new element of divine personality in the world, the personality of God present in the Person of Christ. The arrival of this new element seems consistent with the concept that Evolution is a purposive process driven purposefully forward by the driving force of "radial energy", to use Teilhard's term for the want of a better.

How wise of Christendom to divide all history into BC and AD, because Christ is the hinge on which history turns! The human race is living under new circumstances in the years of Christ! If people were learning before Christ, and the evidence indicates that they were, they are learning too afterwards but in a different way and with a different yardstick. The tragedy is that the human race's learning has been unbalanced. Once it had been woken up by Galileo, it has raced ahead in the fields of science and technology. Yet in the fields of theology and ethics it seems still to be slumbering, frozen into a coma by dogmas which neglect the vitality of Christ's mystical body because of the weight attached to the "canonical" books of the Bible and to the authority of those in charge of the Christian establishment. The living Christ of the Twentieth Century needs to be contemplated in the people in whom He now dwells and whom He motivates; and the development of the Christ of the First Century into the Christ of the Twentieth Century will, I suggest, be more visible if the mystical body is as far as possible viewed as a whole. To view it in all its individual component parts seems impossible, particularly when each part is so fallible and so tainted with sin.

But mention of sin brings me to the problem of good and evil. Hitherto I have considered the concept of Evolution, some mystery of progress from an alpha to an omega, in relation to what I know about Christ and God and Christ's mystical body and have found it compatible with the evidence about all Three. But I have begged the issue of evil and the dark forces which apparently block progress and drag down to nothing so much of what is created. Unless the problem of evil is faced, there is no answer to those who argue that the very harshness of Evolution's struggle for the survival of the fittest is the conclusive argument against a God of Love's being its prime motivator.

Personally it is when I do face up to that problem and consider Christ's message about life and death and heaven and hell, I begin to see more clearly that it is the mystical Christ who provides the evidence that Evolution is indeed God's process and that the historic and living Christ is central to it.

CHAPTER V
The problem of evil

Any concept of creation necessitates some assumption about the concept of nothing and of something. My finite human mind can conceive of a vacuum and has no difficulty about understanding at least the superficialities about material objects. I can see that a table exists; I can touch it and I can knock it and hear it. If I have the right apparatus I can, like a bat, be aware of its existence through some form of radar. I have more difficulty with non-material things, eg electricity and radiation and the personality; but even there my senses confirm their existence and presence, though I should not be able to define the latter, just as I could not define beauty and truth. My mind boggles even more at attempting to understand "nothingness" (I suppose because my mind is a phenomenon which exists), than it does "somethingness"; "being" is easier for me as a concept than "not being".

I see the whole process of being as a tug of war between opposites – "somethingness"; "nothingness"; the positive: the negative; light: darkness: white: black; beauty: ugliness; goodness: badness; joy: pain; truth:

falsehood. In the time span in which I operate on earth I see myself moving forward as it were under the opposing attractions of these poles. Like a pilot steering down a constantly forking river I find myself at every moment forced to decide which fork I am to take and to recollect constantly whether I am heading North or South or East or West.

I suppose because I exist and because I am what I am, I am somehow inexplicably happier with something than with nothing. If personality is the Ground of my Being, and believing as I do in a personal God of love as the Great First Cause, I am obviously happier with the positive poles – light, beauty, goodness, joy and truth; and the negative poles disturb me unpleasantly. I shy away from contemplating nothing and cannot conceive of how the first something could be created out of nothing, even though I can see the products of many artists' attempts at doing that. The mystery of creation is clearly beyond my comprehension; I have to put it on one side and get on with the business of living as creatively as possible.

It is when I do that and come to the exercise of choice that I see that my vision of all the positives is only possible in the context of all the negatives. The pilot of the river steamer could not choose to turn right if the river did not also fork left. Light is only comprehended in darkness, beauty against ugliness, joy against pain and truth against falsehood. I can only choose the good because the evil

The problem of evil

is also there; and if God is my Creator and the source of all being I can only choose Him if the alternative choice of not doing so is open to me. If I am a creature of free will and if I am made in the image of God, then it would seem I must be able to create as God creates and to decide whether to create or not to create; and if I decide not to create but to oppose creation, then I must be using my free will to obstruct what my Creator is doing. Logic can carry me that far but no further. The mystery of good and evil seems wrapped in the mystery of God.

But this is no reason for not making hypotheses, acts of imaginative faith, and seeing how far they fit the facts. The artist to create goes through a painful process. He sees his vision of beauty in his mind's eye but finds himself incapable of producing it. He often struggles and labours and agonises over his creation and often is not satisfied with his final result. The greater the artist, the greater the agony and the ecstasy.

If my hypothesis is correct God, person Who is Love, is creating persons in harmony with Him. To know Him they have to know love and what love experiences. If love (as I can observe in people) creates itself through its own outpouring, God, if love, must do the same on a scale unimaginable to my finite mind. And if agony is part of the process of creation, the agony of God's creation out of nothing must be as unimaginably great as the ecstasy that lies in His achievements. If He wants me to be of His image and at one with Him, He will need to make me capable of doing and experiencing as He does; and everything that Jesus revealed about God suggested that God knows agony in the ecstasy of His creation and that all dealing with the negative is agony for the positive.

Even if it were not so, my knowledge of God and the (in my terms) slow working of His creative process (Evolution) would suggest that the creation of a person of free will would take time and be complicated and involve much joy and agony. The fact that the new person being created was subject to so much tension, pain and grief would be inseparable from the creative process working against the negative: it would not be the purpose and design of God. In one sense therefore the fact that God is Love and acts as Love does can be regarded as the greatest argument for the painful process of Evolution; and it can be argued that had trial and error played no part in it, man could not possibly have been created as person capable of becoming at one with his Creator.

I find that the validity of this argument depends very much on how I regard the problem of evil. If I try to understand the reason for it, I am immediately thrown back on the impossibility of grasping it and the fruitlessness of trying to. But if I start thinking about what I should do about it, my conclusions seem more productive. Indeed the teachings of Jesus and of love seem to supply a simple answer: I shall come to little harm and much wisdom if I welcome my own difficulties and pains as a tempering of the spirit and do my best to alleviate

The problem of evil

those of others. Alas, being fallible and largely unregenerate, I have made and still do make a poor attempt at following that answer. Society contains plenty of people, however, who do much better than I, and I always find knowledge of them both humbling and inspiring, whether they be doctors or nurses, priests or social workers or just good people doing their acts of goodness in their own way. Each adds to my conviction that they provide an answer, while the more obvious saints provide an even more obvious pointer to the answer. Few people must have plunged deeper into sickness, filth and human degradation than Mother Teresa of Calcutta; and what is my faith compared with hers? Whose are the personalities which shine out in the darkness of the world? Faith and love provide an answer; and the fact that those who follow their example gain in their conviction of the rightness of that answer is perhaps the best proof of all.

The counter argument is that Jesus believed a literal interpretation of Jewish tradition as set out in the Old Testament and that no explanation of creation that does not accept the biblical account of sin and the Fall and Christ's atonement can have any validity. Certainly if that is true the theory of Evolution cannot be true and the facts of history do not square with the evidence. All the instincts of my reason tell me to beware of that: and I am made even more cautious by the evident fact of the divisions of opinion among expert theologians. (It is only the theologians of one spectrum who hold to the view that the authority of a literal interpretation of the scriptures is of over-riding authority).

There is therefore nothing in my observation of the problems of pain and evil which conflicts with my hypothesis about Evolution; while my observation of those who tackle the problem with Christian love strengthens my belief that the process is concerned with the creation of personality at one with God's. Does Jesus's teaching about heaven and hell throw more light on my thesis?

CHAPTER VI
Heaven, hell, life and death

In his model prayer Jesus addresses God as "Father in Heaven", and it seems clear that He regarded heaven as where God is. In the old days people thought of the earth as flat and the sky as a great vault with the stars and planets hanging in it and heaven as above the vault and hell as below the earth. Galileo and modern physics have blown that concept to smithereens. But there seems to me one element in it which is still valid – the fact that heaven is above and hell below: not in a spatial sense but in the sense in which, for example, I conceive of a scale of moral values and rate one higher than another. Being in heaven where God is is being in a superior state to being (if that is possible, and I must deal with that later) in hell where God is not.

The Bible contains apocalyptic visions of heaven, and it seems that there was a fashion for writing in apocalyptic terms. Far more important, I suggest, are Jesus's own attempts to describe the kingdom of heaven. The prayer "Thy kingdom come" clearly indicated that He envisaged a time when the Father's kingdom would come. The following phrase "Thy will be done on earth as it is in heaven'' suggests that Jesus saw the establishment of the kingdom of heaven on earth when people carried out God's will and acted in harmony with Him, being at one with Him as Jesus was and still is. The gospels narrate numerous parables through which Jesus tried to get over His concept of the kingdom of heaven and which likened the kingdom both to people and to things, eg his comparing the kingdom to a farmer who sowed his field (Matt XIII), to a mustard seed, to yeast, to hidden treasure, to a net in the sea, to a landowner hiring labourers (Matt XX), to a tyrant throwing a banquet (Matt XXII), to bridesmaids awaiting the groom (Matt XXV), and to an absentee landlord (Matt XXV). These parables are not easy to understand; but the concept of heaven, dealing as it does with what is neither time- nor space-bound, cannot easily be conveyed. Indeed, like the mystic's unitary knowledge of God, knowledge of heaven can, I believe, only really be conveyed by those who are in heaven to those who are there; and the individual's understanding is going to depend on his progress towards attaining the state of being in heaven. Knowing how far I am from that state I cannot look to myself for an answer. And so I am thrown back again on Jesus and the conclusion that heaven must be a state of harmony with God, and an individual's progress towards heaven his progress in developing his relationship with God into that state of harmony.

The fact that Jesus said "I tell you truly, there are some

standing here who will not taste death before they see the kingdom of God" (Luke IX 27) suggests that Jesus saw that something was going to happen soon, and it did: His death, His resurrection, the coming of the Holy Spirit and the creation of His mystical body. It all fits together. If the individual is, as a believing Christian, part of Christ's mystical body and if he is wholly at one with Christ in that body, then he must also be at one with God and therefore in heaven, albeit still in his physical immature state which will become mature once he has passed through death.

My brief glance at the problem of pain and evil noted that I could not conceive of white without black and good without bad; and the same seems to be true of heaven. To conceive of heaven where God is, I must conceive of hell where God is not; and I must try to imagine being urged towards a nothingness where separation from God is total. My imagination balks at such an attempt, and I find myself repelled. Is there any alternative I can consider which may provide a background against which more dimly to perceive something of heaven. I think there is in the state of those who deliberately set themselves against God, who deliberately exercise their power of free will (of choice) to obstruct the power of love, who want to negate against God rather than create with Him.

Whether or not there is a personal devil like the Mephistopheles of Goethe, "Ich bin der Geist der stets verneint" (I am the spirit who for ever negates) I do not know. But it does seem as if, as time goes by, the collective memory of people and their interaction on each other does create an almost palpable influence, a sort of collective personality. Really wicked people seem to create a sort of collective personality of evil which balefully influences those who deliberately relate to it. For me that devil is obvious, active and dangerous. And if the phenomenon of personality is indeed capable of existence beyond the body's death, and if it continues to operate between the poles of God and nothing, there is something horrifying about being excluded by choice from the Being that is. As individuals are perhaps as rarely wholly bad as they are saints at one with God, I imagine that most will not be wholly set against the power of love when they die and that thereafter through perhaps some painful process of atonement they will be drawn into that state of harmony for which they were created. But if individuals are genuinely to have freedom of choice, they must be set free to choose between heaven and hell, and some presumably do choose the latter. I cannot judge the state of other people because I do not know their most secret motives; nor do I know the other circumstances which are influencing their choice. What I can see is the important effect which choice has on an individual's relationships.

The thought that what happens to an individual at the moment of death may depend on his relationship to God at that moment is to me particularly alarming and

Heaven, Hell, life and death

uncomfortable! If by my conduct I have so reduced the divine spark of love with which I was endowed at birth that there is no love and nothing in me which the love of God can grasp, what will prevent me from going to the nothingness or limbo to which my rejection of love will impel me?

Better by far to be snuffed out than to suffer eternally in a limbo of rejection by my own will. But will the love-rejecting be snuffed out? Christ was clear that they would not be.

Acceptance of the fact of Jesus's resurrection involves acceptance of after life; and Jesus clearly believed that there is a separation in after life between those in harmony with God and those out of harmony. His teaching about life and death seems clear: "God so loved the world that He gave His Son so that everyone who believes in Him...may have eternal life" (John III 16). "I tell you most solemnly, whoever listens to my words and believes in the one who sent me has eternal life" (John V 24).

Life is a state of being the fullness of which depends on the individual's harmony with God. If there is no harmony and the individual totally rejects God there is in effect no life in him. Jesus said enough about the miseries of hell where those suffer who are rejected by God to indicate that He saw something in time-terms indestructible about personality; and I find the concept of a personality's becoming nothing as difficult as the concept of a nothing in which God is ever creating something.

What does, however, seem important about a consideration of heaven and hell and life and death is that it leads, in the light of Jesus, to a supposition that these unsatisfactory and inadequate words are all about a state of being of people which depends on their relationship with God, and that this relationship is in one sense developing as their collective awareness of God develops and in another sense is unchangingly dependent on the way in which they exercise their free will. In that free will is an attribute of the phenomenon of the human species, sin (the conscious opposing and rejecting of God) must have come into the world with the appearance of man; but consideration of its appearance and of the process of overcoming it to achieve an at-onement with God falls into the following chapter. Suffice it to conclude here that a Christian concept of heaven and hell and of death and life does not conflict with the hypothesis that Evolution is God's process for the generation of personality at one with His.

CHAPTER VII
Evolution and atonement

At first sight there seems to be an irrefutable contradiction between the concept of Evolution and Christian concepts of man's fall from grace (his falling out of a state of harmony with God) and atonement through Christ's sacrifice on the cross. People nowadays know enough about animal behaviour to see that in his ignorance and simplicity primitive man was much more akin to the mammals of his day than is the human race of to-day and that his moral concepts were undeveloped. Survival to him involved very different considerations and judgments than it does to me. His freedom of choice and his ability to ponder and reflect were much more circumscribed by his circumstances than mine are by mine; but within his narrow limits, unlike the species before him, he did have a moral choice and how he exercised it influenced his relationships with God. That relationship must have governed his state of being on earth and, if the personality after death timelessly continues, affected its afterlife. Under the surge of his animalian instincts, lust, greed and the basic desires of the flesh may have loomed larger on his horizons than the corresponding virtues, but the force of love which had brought him into being none the less played upon him and drew him forward. The first conscious choice set him on a path between the poles of light and darkness veering from side to side, developing a relationship with both and slowly contributing to a collective consciousness which would grow in influence as time wore on. Thus, through the misuse of free will, was born in all the trend to sin which later generations (typical of the individual's tendency to blame his faults on someone else) blamed on a common ancestor Adam.

As society developed so hierarchies grew, rulers came and went, laws were laid down and justice was administered. Just as the offending child came to expect the smack of retribution so too in a well-run society the criminal, if discovered, expected punishment and, like the smarting child, thought that the punishment had largely if not completely expiated the offence. Ancestor worship and the prevailing dread of tyrants must have helped in the minds of ordinary people the attribution of human qualities to the public's concept of God; and, in so far as rulers and priests coincided or worked hand in glove together their interests probably seemed best served by concepts of God in their image. It is not hard to imagine how in such circumstances people came to think of God as some being of arbitrary anger, rage and vindictiveness who was best appeased by flattery and sacrificial gifts. Human and later other sacrifices and in the early days of Israel the practice of the scape-goat can

Evolution and atonement

all be seen as attempts to attribute to the demands of God man's inherited bad conscience and subconscious desire for expiation for bad thoughts and deeds. It is noteworthy that, as the Jews came to understand God a little better, their more enlightened seers realised that God demanded service rather than sacrifice, love rather than expiation.

It is inconceivable that a God of love would require His Son to suffer the agonies of the cross to propitiate Himself. The propitiation seems rather to have been man's demand put into the mouth of the God of his imagining by ignorance and wilful misunderstanding. In His agonised prayer before His arrest Jesus accepted that God's way of love necessitated that He accept the worst that man could do to Him in order to break the causal chain of evil; and He established the rule of love by ending the tyranny of sin with its legacy of desire for expiation through yet more evil.

So the greatest evil that man could do led to the greatest good that God could do. Thereafter man could regard himself as free both of his own sin and of the collective sin of the whole human race if only he entered into and accepted the sacrifice of Jesus, who in His sinless humanity had fully expiated sinning humanity's offence. It is through acceptance of that sacrifice and through both absorbing and becoming absorbed by the personality of Christ that the individual is brought back into harmony with God into that state of "at-onement" for which he was designed.

Thus Jesus's sacrifice and atonement on the cross seem to me fully consistent with God's love working through a process of Evolutionary development of the human personality.

CHAPTER VIII
The Individual

Gone are the days when it was theoretically possible for one individual to grasp the sum of human knowledge. Now knowledge is growing at a frightening speed, perhaps doubling in one or two decades all that has gone before. No longer is it possible for one individual to grasp the sum of knowledge even in certain sectors and so the individual's fields of specialisation seem to be growing ever narrower. I have known for a long time that an Einstein can be a duffer on the football field and a disaster in the kitchen; and experience has taught me both my own fallibility and the fallibility of others. Like Fitzgerald:

"Myself when young did eagerly frequent
Doctor and Saint, and heard great argument
About it and about: but evermore
Came out by the same door where in I went."

Unlike Omar Khayyam, however, I did not turn to pleasure and the bottle because hedonism seemed not to provide a satisfying answer: there seems no lasting satisfaction to be had in placating the desires of the flesh and the attempt to satisfy them generally ruins the flesh. It was not the argument of the Saint which appealed but his personality which inspired; and so, as a Christian, I found myself evermore thrown back on Christ. The answer seemed to lie with Him.

He not only talked about life but He talked about the sustenance to maintain spiritual life. Physically He needed a minimum of food and drink like anyone else. Spiritually He also needed food and drink, and the fourth gospel is remarkably specific about what He regarded as spiritual food and drink. "My food is to do the will of the one who sent me" (John IV 34); and in the same chapter John concludes from Jesus's remarks to the Samaritan woman that the drink about which He was talking and of which He had drunk in His moment of quiet communion with God by the well side was the refreshment that comes from communion (prayer and meditation) with God:

"If you only knew what God is offering and who it is that is saying to you: give me a drink, you would have been the one to ask, and He would have given you living water…Whoever drinks this (natural) water will get thirsty again; but anyone who drinks the water that I shall give will never be thirsty again: the water that I shall give will turn into a spring inside him, welling up to eternal life."

Later in his sixth chapter John indicated that Jesus expanded on this with teaching so hard to understand that it drove people away.

"I am the bread of life….I am the living bread

The individual

that comes...from heaven so that a man may eat it and not die...the bread that I shall give is my flesh...I tell you most solemnly if you do not eat the flesh of the Son of Man and drink his blood you will not have life in you. Anyone who does eat my flesh and drink my blood has eternal life...for my flesh is real food and my blood is real drink. He who eats my flesh and drinks my blood lives in me and I live in him."

Only after Jesus's death, resurrection, ascension and the coming of the Holy Spirit did his closest followers begin to understand what He had been driving at.

As Christ's mystical body of individuals with faith in Him grew, so it seems to me the importance of the Eucharist – the recelebration of Jesus's sacrifice on the cross – has also grown. In the same way, when I bother to celebrate the Eucharist properly in a right frame of mind and with more than my average concentration of will and mind, it seems to grow in importance to me, and I draw new sustenance and inspiration from it. By letting God's love draw me into a sharing of Christ's physical experience – His experience on earth both in his physical and his mystical body – and in his spiritual experience in both too, I find myself refreshed and revived in some mysterious way, the mystery of which seems akin to all my awe and sense of mystery in approaching the Absolute.

When I am inspired by other people I find that what

inspires me is not the product of my cool and rational assessment of their personality. It is rather a warm sense of intuitive attraction which draws me to something about them, something about the way they are and what they do. That most attractive of saints, Francis of Assisi, is reported to have addressed the crowds as "Good people" not because he thought that they were necessarily good – most crowds are not – but because he saw in each individual the divine spark in that wonderful phenomenon made in God's image, and saw more clearly than I shall ever see what that spark could become if only the individual would wholly surrender to Christ. Just as most people develop their physical senses by using them, so it seems do individuals develop their spiritual senses by using them. The more I look for Christ in others, the more I find Him there. The more I look at Christ as revealed in those in whom He dwells, the better do I see Him as He is. The more I contemplate His mystical body, the more I see there is to contemplate and the more the inspiration I draw from that contemplation. The more I enter others' communion with Him the more I enter into His communion with the Father.

There is a remarkable contrast between that sort of experience and other sorts. If I increase my knowledge through book learning, I find myself becoming imprisoned in the narrowness of my specialisation and arrogant in my superior knowledge. If I excel at a sport, the winning inflates my ego. But with seeking Christ the

The individual

reverse is true. The more I see Him in His saints, the dimmer the light in which I view myself. The more clearly I perceive Him directly, the more awe-struck I am by what He is and the greater the sense of my own impurity and insignificance. I feel that, if I really came face to face with Him, my sense of shame would make me want to run away: only such bonds of love as I had allowed to grow would hold me to Him. And this would be even truer in the direct presence of God unveiled. There only Christ could hold me; and if Christ had nothing He could catch hold of in me, I would run away and be lost of my own volition.

There are those who see in a theory of evolution a belief that as communications improve, population increases and the world shrinks in the mind of man, the development of a collective memory is going to lead to the development of a collective personality which will snuff out the individual and collectivise the human will. That belief does not, on my observation of progress over the past two thousand years and of the circumstances of today, fit the facts as they are; nor does it fit the hypothesis which I have argued.

What does seem true is that if individuals *do* do what Christ instructed – if they take the drink of communion with God and the food of doing the Father's will – they do see more clearly the truth of Christianity, and they sense faith strengthened, hope brightened and love increased; and they view life as the life of Christ's developing mystical body of which they are in their individuality an integral part, with an individual contribution to make to the working and effectiveness of the whole. Far from Christianity's involving the negation of individuality, it seems to involve the fulfilment of the individual through harmony with God.

CHAPTER IX
Vocation and the priest

Thanks to the Marxist view that religion is dope for the masses the term vocation is often associated with a class conscious attitude to society: all have their proper place in society and ought to stay there. That, however, seems a wholly unchristian view of society.

For a Christian believer the truly Christian society is the mystical body of Christ, the framework of relationships which ties every individual in whom Christ dwells into a comprehensive whole – a form of society which exists in the earth-bound society of the world and yet is separate and distinct from it. In that society it is the individual's relationship with God through Jesus that counts. Some are getting closer to Him, some are drifting away. Faith and love hold people in, while a rejection of faith and love pushes them out. Those outside who have never been brought into contact with Christ are still only able to grope for the truth like their ancestors before Christ's revelation. Those who have been brought into contact with Christ but are outside because of neglect or deliberate intention seem in much worse condition, for they are actively rejecting Christ and membership of His mystical body.

The jobs people do in life seem of no importance compared with the extent to which they dwell in and are indwelt by Christ and to which others catch Christ's personality from theirs. All in Christ's mystical body seem equal in their original capacity to achieve a state of harmony with God; they differ in their progress towards it, and the jobs they do may help or hinder their progress.

What people do must depend to a large extent upon their circumstances and individual talents; but some choice is usually open and whatever the job, unless it is fundamentally evil and contrary to the God of Love, it will provide scope in the way in which it is done to achieve progress in Christ. The saint who like Theresa of Lisieux does every task, however humble, to the glory of God is at the top of the list and in heaven, while the millionaire whose mind is obsessed by acquisitiveness may be at the bottom and on his way to hell. The more attuned individuals are to the voice of God in Christ the more clearly will they sense their vocation and choose the job or jobs for which they were designed; and it seems reasonable that the job intended for them may indeed change as they grow and develop in spirit, experience and capability.

For members of Christ's mystical body there does, however, seem to be one sector of employment – that of the priest and the religious – where special circumstances apply. If they are certain that they are called to that way

Vocation and the priest

of life, people are choosing to be in some special way the mediators of Christ to their fellow individuals. By their vows and ordination they are set apart in the noblest but also the most difficult walks of life; and their chosen expertise based on the example of their Master, Christ, is to mediate God to others through the religious rites which they specialise in conducting and through what they can teach as a result of their expertise in prayer and meditation and the Christian way of life. So long as they are priests it would seem both right and logical that they should regard themselves and be regarded as set apart. There is an obvious danger in their involving themselves or claiming an expertise in the lowlier and earthier occupations of their flock: either they will lose respect by revealing their ignorance and naivety or they will be tempted to brand honest differences of opinion as immoral and unchristian when in actuality the reverse may be true. Christ Himself, according to all that is known about Him, steadfastly refused to criticise or involve Himself in the state or the economic or social conditions of His day. His concern was with revealing God and leading people into harmony with Him; and his challenge to the religious establishment of His day was based on that establishment's failure in its religious duty.

The pattern of evolution would suggest that the priesthood like everything else would be subject to progress and to occasional set-backs on its way forward. The pattern of human behaviour would also suggest that individual priests would be fallible. Indeed in their case pride would seem an especial danger, for it is easy for the priest to see himself in God, to believe that his voice is God's and thus to wreak havoc in God's name. History is full of ghastly crimes committed in the name of Christ! These are an awful warning against allowing the religious establishment too much authority and power. On the other hand the way in which the Christian church has grown and developed is a tribute to its leadership as a whole down the past twenty centuries and evidence that Christ is indeed alive in His mystical body. Nor does His intervention in the affairs of man, through those in whom He dwells, seem other than God's intervention through the forward impetus of love in the process of Evolution. Thus to answer to a call of God is to work with God's tide of Evolution; to refuse it is to swim against that tide. Vocation is not the chain that binds the individual to the status quo; it is the call that summons him or her out to meet the challenge of opportunity and of the possibility of self-fulfilment in the personality of Christ.

CHAPTER X

Prayer

It is not my purpose to discuss the role of prayer in Evolution and some would deny that prayer could have had any effect compatible with what we know about Evolution, for to ask God to intervene against His laws of nature would be to ask Him to be untrue to His own nature and to negate man's free will and thus to defeat His own purposes.

According to the gospels Jesus set great store by prayer and drew life from His communion with the Father. He underlined the importance of asking and promised that whatever His followers asked in His name would be granted and He left behind not only His model Lord's Prayer but also examples of how He prayed. To pray in his name, ie under His inspiration, I need to enter into His mind both directly and indirectly through the corporate mind of His mystical body and those individuals in whom He has dwelt. The process of that sort of communion with God seems to be a process of holding myself up to the radiance of God's love so as to become irradiated by it; and the process of praying for others seeks to hold them up likewise. The phenomenon of telepathy, the way in which one personality can influence another and the evidence of the power of prayer in others, are all evidence that prayer does work, just as the failure of my praying is evidence of my weakness. Nor does there seem anything contrary to the exercise of free will in prayer: if it intensifies the power of love by reflecting God's love through numerous personalities, it is in effect the way in which one individual working with God of his own free will can help bring forward the day when those who do not reject God become at one with Him. Prayer is not only compatible with Evolution, it is the individual's attempt to harness himself to the driving force of Evolution.

CHAPTER XI
The Future

When I look at the world's underside, everywhere I see the negative – poverty, degradation, disease, disaster, crime, terrorism and all the other elements of negation – and I dally with despair. When I try to put myself behind the eyes of Jesus I see it with a texture shot through with love like a piece of dark textile shot through with gold thread: everywhere in all sorts of unlikely people love seems energetically active in creation. I look at Evolution in the time context of the evanescent bacterium and see nothing; but in the context of the time-span of the human personality some progress is visible. In the untold millenia before Christ people had developed to a point of inter-dependence and inter-communication which had brought about a collective memory and some form of corporate personality. With Christ a new phenomenon, His mystical body, appeared; and in the comparatively short period of two thousand years it has grown enormously, developing both a collective memory and a collective personality. Though greatly troubled by the errors and weaknesses of its component people, including both leaders and led, it does seem to have moved forward. In total more people have achieved a state of unitary knowledge of God through Christ and more people have made progress in that direction; and their activity has led to a strengthening of the power of love pulling people in that direction. At the same time the tug in the opposite direction has increased. It is almost as if, as the one force increases, so too does the opposite, just as the forces of electricity build up until the strength is reached where the lightning bolt breaks down the resistance of the separating elements. Perhaps the omega point of evolution will be like that, and in the twinkling of an eye the process of at-onement will be complete. The mystics' experience of the searing flame of unitary knowledge of God suggests that the simile of lightning is perhaps better than any other to describe something indescribable in human terms.

Nor do I need to describe it. Whatever it will be, I can do nothing positive about it except help it on its way by adding my potential to the energy driving towards it. And even then what can I a single lay person do? The legend of Pope Innocent III's dream provides an encouraging answer: he woke up dreaming that the fabric of St Peter's Rome was cracking and that only the efforts of a small individual was supporting the pillars and preventing the church from falling down. Francis of Assisi did have an astounding effect on the church and still has, being perhaps the best-loved saint of all. And does not my own experience confirm that answer. From whom have I most

The Future

caught the personality of Christ – from the prelates and the powerful rich and important people with whom I have had contact, or from some of the seemingly least significant? The latter is surely true.

And so my vision of the progress towards the consummation of the Creator's purpose in His creation, is the vision of the progress of innumerable people moving towards a state of "eternal life" in harmony with God through conscious communion with Him through Christ and through constant attempts to act in accordance with His will. And at bottom, when I regard this vision, I know what I should do, even if, far more than Saint Paul, I experience that what in my wisdom I would do in my weakness I generally do not and vice versa. Indeed the knowledge of what I should do strengthens my conviction that the only possibility of doing it lies in surrender to the personality of Christ, so that I do it through Him and He does it through me.

Thus, through Christ, I am back where I started with God with Whom I saw Evolution begin and in Whom I see it ending. My original hypothesis holds good, and it is the only one which seems to provide meaning and coherence to the circumstances in which, in being, I find myself.

Part II

CHAPTER XII

The Christian Clerical Establishments

Over thirty years of experience in a state establishment has given me a profound mistrust of all establishments. The trouble with them is that they condition their servants to become "establishment people", restrained in a straitjacket woven out of their particular establishment's collective thinking and traditions and the self-serving interests which they share with their establishment as a corporate whole. Religious establishments seem among the most untrustworthy of all, because they claim both the backing of God and to speak for God and thereby develop an almost unique arrogance. Being longer-lasting than most establishments religious establishments become even more ensnared in their bigotry, jargon and precedents. It was no accident that caused Christ to lambast the Jewish establishment in His day; nor was it by accident that that establishment had Him killed; or that many martyrs infected by Christ and inspired by the

Honest to Christ

Holy Spirit were subsequently done to death by Christian church establishments down the ages.

Apart from the inherent fallibility of all human establishments another reason for this misguided slaughter seems the failure of Christian leaders to accept that God is primarily concerned with the individual. Human personality is of its nature individual: God's love is transmitted through individuals, the Holy Spirit inspires individuals, and it is Christ-infected individuals who compose the mystical body of Christ. There are more nominal Christians alive to-day than have ever been alive at one time. It is therefore not unreasonable to assume that Christ's mystical body of true believers is more vigorous than it has ever been. Looking at the Christian laity throughout the world, I think it is. I see no evidence to suggest that Christendom which has existed for nearly 2000 years will not continue to go on growing. But over those years there have been many crises in its leadership.

I sense now a general malaise about the Christian clergy and see signs that another major crisis comparable to the Reformation is abrewing. The tensions seem of two kinds.

First there is the tension between the laity and the clergy. Whereas in medieval times the clergy had the brains and one of the best routes to preferment for the common-born was a career in the church, now business and the so-called secular professions attract the best brains and the most prestige. The traditional paternal attitudes of the clergy towards the laity are thus out of place and resented and increase the divide between the clerical establishment and the secular world, including the Christian laity. Nor are the laity prepared to accept the sterile concepts of obedience to authority which enabled church leaders to perpetrate the horrors that many of them have over the past two millenia done in the name of Christ. Unfortunately the spectacle of the Church of Rome's convening of a Council on the Role of the Laity in whose deliberations the laity were allowed no effective participation has not lessened this tension. Nor has the hypocrisy of the Anglican establishment over synodical government: while ostensibly giving the laity a voice in church government this "reform" in practice gives the laity no real power but transfers additional power to the bishops. And every parson who makes it clear to his parochial church council that the laity are only there to do the chores while leaving policy to him still further aggravates the tension.

The second source of tension lies in the cultural divide between the clergy and the secular world. Steeped in the imagery and language of the Bible, the clergy tend to speak in terms no longer relevant to the laity and often incomprehensible to those outside the church. The clergy tend to live in the past, to fear change and to hang back from embracing the opportunities which the future offers. The secular world on the other hand tends to be motivated by people of optimism and initiative, eager to take advantage of science and technology and to plan for the future.

To the lay eye the effect of these tensions appears sadly visible in at least three of the main Christian churches. In the church of Rome there are strains between the Pope and the curia on the one hand and the mass of the faithful on the other: in the face of modern science and technology and over-population the bulk of the Roman Catholic laity will not accept the church's teaching on, for example, birth control and abortion; and the bishops in the field are harried by both sides. In the Baptist churches there is schism between the conservative anti-scientific fundamentalists who believe in the literal truth of every word in the Bible and those who adopt a more liberal scientific stance. Both intrigue against each other while a new generation of TV gospel-preachers by their personal conduct and money-grubbing propaganda risk giving a bad name to all types of mass-evangelisation. The Anglican church seems paralysed by a failure of leadership: the bishops seem eager to pronounce on political, social and economic issues where they have no particular expertise by virtue of their office but fight shy of coming off the fence where issues such as sexual morals or the role of women are concerned.

In the face of this potentially explosive situation I suggest that the leaders of the church establishments need to review their organisation, teaching and practices in the context of the world as it now is and seems likely to

The Christian Clerical Establishments

become, if the pattern of current trends continues. My personal conclusions on the implications of accepting my hypothesis about Evolution suggest that our Christian clergy could well start by publicly accepting that hypothesis and proceeding from there. In the following chapters I put forward a number of Aunt Sallies for them to knock down or adopt.

CHAPTER XIII
The Role of the Clergy

As individuals members of the clergy are like any other individual Christians: they proceed through life reacting in one way or another to God's love and to a greater or less extent allowing themselves to become infected by the personality of Christ and inspired by the Holy Spirit. Like most other Christians in this life the clergy mostly do not succeed in being totally taken over by Christ and being brought by Him into a state of harmony with God; and self continues to prevent their reaching that state of unity with God which God wills for everyone. The clergy differ only from the laity in that they have accepted as their vocation a career of special service in Christ's mystical body of believers. That service is to mediate between God and the people: through the sacraments and their service to disseminate God's love, spread the infection of Christ's personality and help people to become more receptive to the inspiration of the Holy Spirit. To enable them to carry out their vocation they have conferred upon them the privilege of performing the sacramental ceremonies and are through ordination given a special measure of help (grace) to enable them to be effective in their priestly role. Because they are devoting their career to their priestly task, they should be able to develop an expertise in the functioning of Christ's mystical body which is not normally obtainable by those engaged in other occupations. (I have carefully avoided putting the adjective "secular" before "occupations" since I do not accept that there is that distinction between the occupations of the clergy and the laity: if individuals are infected by Christ and inspired by the Holy Spirit and let Christ and the Holy Spirit motivate them in the careers to which they have been called, their activities will become an integral part of God's design and as much in accordance with God's creative purposes as those of the clergy).

As with other occupations the rapid growth of knowledge and the increasing complication of society brought about by advances in science and technology force upon individual clergy the need to specialise. Prayer, meditation and contemplation are activities in which all Christians need to engage; but the clergy should by devoting more concentrated effort to them know more about their techniques and be able out of the greater depth of their experience to counsel at least those members of the laity who desire to improve their performance. Judging by the clergy in the pulpits of the churches which I have frequented, I have the impression that protestant theological colleges devote far too little attention to this aspect of Christian living and must sadly record how little help I have personally received from the clergy in this.

It is probably a truism to say that Christ is caught rather than taught. By studying Him as He is revealed in the New Testament we can learn about Him as we learn about the Roman Emperors by studying the Roman history of the period. But it is by imaginatively contemplating Him as He was and as He, the risen Christ, is in every individual in whom he dwells that we are really captivated by Him. There is nothing static about the risen Christ, because He expresses Himself through the lives of people developing in a developing society. We see Him at work in people such as Francis of Assisi, Thomas More, Pascal, John Wesley, Mother Teresa and the unknown neighbour who exudes His personality in his or her quiet faith and love-dominated existence; and the odds are that we catch Christ most easily from those infected by Him in our immediate circle at work or play. Yet having caught Christ from someone, we need to deepen the infection and subject ourselves to the influence of those who have let Christ operate most powerfully through their personality. Here the clergy seem to fail most dismally; and by and large their sermons and conversation show little trace of their being captivated by the Christ of individual "saints". Far more relevant than biblical criticism would seem the study of Christ at work in the "saints" and the development of His mystical body in the corps of all believers. Would not the theologians be better occupied with that than with their tedious and irrelevant debates about scripture and doctrine?

Individuals are infinite in their variety but nevertheless hold many traits in common. Some personalities have a particular appeal to others; and there would seem considerable merit in seeking to classify the recognized Christian "saints" so that people seeking to be more deeply infected by them with Christ could most rapidly be directed towards the most appropriate saints. Here modern computer techniques should prove helpful; but it will also be necessary to produce material on the saints in a form suitable for prayerful meditation where the operation of Christ within the "saint" is high-lighted and themes for meditation are isolated in such a way as to maximise the infecting and inspiring process. Books of starter-meditations and prayer on the lives of individual "saints" would, I suggest, be far more conducive to helpful and imaginative meditation than the Bible-reading leaflets now prepared by many church organisations.

We live in a world that is rapidly shrinking as communications improve. Already the media have brought the world into the sitting-room; and the rapidly spreading use of English as to-day's language of science and technology and probably to-morrow's recognised global language is for good and ill breaking down the boundaries of separate cultures. Being in the business of communication the clergy cannot ignore these modern trends: to be effective they must needs develop an

The Role of the Clergy

expertise in modern methods and learn particularly from other professions. (In this area too I am constantly struck by the amateurism of the clergy: whereas advertising companies are constantly checking the effects of their methods and messages, the clergy by and large seem disinterested; and I am never asked by a preacher what I thought of his sermon. Nor am I conscious that the Anglican establishment, for example, is really bothered about getting the Christian message over or genuinely worried about its dwindling influence on a growing population).

In the preceding chapter I remarked on the divide between paternal priests and the laity and the apparent unwillingness to regard the laity as partners in Christ's mystical body. Though similes are rarely wholly accurate, there does seem to be a similarity between a parish family of people and an orchestra. The people are like the players: each has a particular instrument to play and a distinctive contribution to make. The music they want to play is God's music. To play it they need a conductor who will manage them and direct their playing and enable them to their best capacity to play what the composer really had in mind. Yet the clergy reveal little evidence of training in the management of time and talents and by and large seem uninterested in calling on the talents of their flock, particularly where these may underscore their own lack of talent. I suspect that the clergy would find their role infinitely more effective and rewarding if

Honest to Christ

they would think of themselves more as manager members of a team rather than doers on their own; and I am sure that they would gain thereby much respect from the laity. Moreover, by drawing the laity more closely into the activity of the church, the clergy would be increasing greatly the laity's commitment.

When I was a boy I was told that the church was exciting. It was no doubt my fault that I have never found it so. Yet the concept of God's working His creative plans out through Evolution is intensely exciting. Here I am a member of His resurrected Son's mystical body, alive at a time when the human race is almost daily gaining more capacity both to control its environment and its own development – a time when science and technology are advancing with dizzying speed! I want to hang on and hold tight and face the future with the confidence that is born of faith in God's design and in His mysterious processes; and I want the clergy to catch the exhilaration and eagerly drive forward too. To do that they need to pin their faith on the evolving mystical body in which the resurrected Christ lives and to concentrate on its adaptation to developing circumstances.

That process of adaptation will require new attitudes and probably involve much contention. On this I will now touch in the following chapter.

CHAPTER XIV

The Adaptation of Christ's Mystical Body to Changing Circumstances

If the pattern of Evolution is one of adaptation and survival, it seems not unreasonable to assume that the relatively new phenomenon of Christ's mystical body is going to fit into the process too, particularly if the whole process is part of God's design for the human race. The fact that through science and technology mankind is increasingly able to influence its own development and change its environment adds to its responsibility, which is growing all the time: we have the power to destroy ourselves and our immediate environment; and we can resist God's creative purposes in ways inconceivable in the past. This underlines for us Christians the importance of being active members of Christ's mystical body so that we can create in cooperation with God and not negate in opposition to Him. Nor should we forget that the criteria of active membership are the extent to which we, as individuals, absorb and are absorbed by the personality of Christ and inspired by the Holy Spirit. Christ and the

Holy Spirit and the love of the unchanging Father are the constants in the equation of our circumstances; and those constants, if we let them, can alone enable the human race to use correctly its new powers to change mankind and its environment and to adapt correctly to survive and ultimately attain the end for which it was designed.

I am sceptical that governments of themselves possess any divine authority, though they are naturally mostly only too willing to claim it. What divine authority they do enjoy must, I suggest, flow from the extent to which those who wield the power are divinely inspired. Church establishments long to subject governments to their influence. What they should be seeking is to infect the population with Christ and to encourage committed Christians to play their part in politics. Only in that way will the machinery of government become through the people who comprise it infected with Christ and inspired by the Holy Spirit. And it will be those people, not the priesthood, who will hold effective political power.

Laws and traditions and customs are all man-made and usually designed to preserve human society and adapt it to changing circumstances. (We would do well to remember that the new-born baby is created by God with no rights – only an absolute dependence on the love of others). Being man-made laws, traditions and customs, are, however wise or divinely inspired, subject to the effects of time and change; and societies which have not adapted them to changing circumstances have generally not survived and will not survive. I have in the first part of this book shown how acceptance of my hypothesis about Evolution leads the Christian to accept that ultimately the divine plan can be achieved only in and through Christ. Bearing in mind Christ's teaching about the innate conflict between the spirit and the flesh, we have to examine our spiritual and physical circumstances as they are and tune our laws, traditions and customs to the needs of the moment. In those circumstances moral issues take on a new complexity.

In a primitive society with high death rates and a need of every pair of hands that can survive birth control may make little sense. In an over-populated country with diminishing resources and falling living-standards birth control may prove the only course of action for survival. Nor should the quality of life be disregarded. God must have given individuals their talents and capabilities to be used to the maximum in His creative process. Grinding poverty and inadequate food destroys capabilities and prevents talents from being developed. A mother may need to be protected against an over-demanding husband from unwanted pregnancies if she is to have the strength, time and resources to give her children a decent start on their Christian pilgrimage. Advances in medical knowledge and ability to combat disease need also to be taken into account in determining the ethics of birth control which, Evolution could yet record, may be an essential element in God's creative plan.

Rights over life and death could reasonably be regarded as the prerogative of God before people had any control over their lives. In the old days it was the executioners who tried to prolong the lives of their victims in order to extract the maximum suffering before death terminated their torture. Today it is often our doctors who officiously prolong the lives of the aged, injured and grievously handicapped and condemn them to maybe years of physical and mental degradation and pain. Thou shalt not kill nor strive officiously to keep alive may be a good precept for the doctor; but it evades the moral problems which progress has thrust upon us. Christian societies have traditionally condemned suicide but praised self-sacrifice. Captain Oates was regarded as heroic for walking out into the snow in a useless attempt to save his colleagues in the Antarctic; and all who give their lives to save others are usually admired. In Eskimo tribes it was the accepted custom for the aged to walk out to death in the snow; if the hunting failed and food was insufficient for the family. In these days when the body can be kept alive long after the human personality appears to have lost all control over itself and when the individual has apparently permanently lost consciousness, the question becomes insistent whether this is right. With doctors now capable of forecasting with reasonable accuracy the progress of disease and of transplanting organs as vital as the heart and lungs, the question will soon become topical whether patients should be permitted to give their vital organs to help others to survive who would have with those organs the prospect of a creative future, and to decide to die early while still capable of taking a conscious and responsible decision. The limitless cost of medical services seems also likely to force upon society a selection of priorities which will inevitably raise contentious moral issues. If resources are limited, should they be concentrated where they can do most good for the greatest number of people? Does society owe the right of life as much to the grievously handicapped as to those capable of life to the full? In the interests of the former should the latter be deprived of resources which they need to develop their full potential? The time is surely coming when people will become even more god-like in their control over life and death, the course of pregnancies, genes, sex, brain development etc. To turn our backs on progress would be to contract out of the evolutionary process and to turn our backs on God. We can draw comfort from our knowledge that Christ and the Holy Spirit have guided Christ's mystical body through two thousand years of changing and developing circumstances and that Christ and the Holy Spirit are there to guide us through the moral maze ahead. How They have done that guiding in the past through the people whom They have been able the most effectively to work through must provide the best pointer to how They will do it in the future.

It is an old adage that good cases make bad law; and religious establishments have set much store on the need to preserve their law. But the whole point of Christ's entry into the world was to provide Himself to supersede law. He revealed that God is a God of Love Who is concerned with love not law. He taught that God wants people to live in harmony with Him and His creative purposes; and that through the action of the Holy Spirit people can become at one with God by letting themselves absorb and be absorbed by His (Christ's) personality. By His perfectly lived life on earth He made Himself the proper yard stick of human conduct. By the way in which He has been absorbed by and absorbed Christians down the ages He has provided the models of human conduct and set forth ideals against which people can measure themselves and to which they can aspire. We all fall short of those ideals because we all fail to let Jesus and the Holy Spirit take us over. We hope that the clergy will help us to see those ideals a little clearer and to do a little better in our attempts to attain them. We can leave it to governments to frame the laws needed for the regulation of society and in democracies, where we have a meaningful vote and the power to influence governmental decisions, do our best through the machinery of the state to see that the law is compatible with what we believe is God's design.

To sum up the preoccupations which I have touched

upon in this chapter seem to me to be some of the real issues which should be engaging the minds of our prelates – not the political and economic issues to which they at present devote so much attention.

CHAPTER XV
1988 – A Year of Crisis

1987 seems likely to go down in history as a bad year for both the Roman Catholic and Baptist religious establishments. With its damp squib of a Council on the Role of the Laity the former lost a major opportunity to lessen the tensions within the Church of Rome and to speed up its overdue adaptation to the circumstance which will surround the two thousandth anniversary of its founding. With the Bakker scandal and the jockeying for power in its national and state organisations the American Baptists experienced erosion in their predominant influence on television in the Southern States and a deepening of the strife between the fundamentalists and their opponents. Nor did in its autumn synod the papering over of deep divisions within the Church of England reflect much credit on its leadership. The signs are that 1988 is going to be potentially an even more important year for the Christian religion.

To begin with the Communist atheist countries are in their own crises of adaptation. In the Soviet Union the Marxist philosophy has already proved intellectually bankrupt; not even the members of the Politburo seem now to believe that it can deliver on its economic promises or provide any real hope of achieving a society in which individuals can experience the freedom and opportunity to fulfil their potential. Against well dug-in opposition within the party establishment Mr Gorbachov is trying to do the impossible: to impose adaptation from the top down without weakening the structure of the party or the authority of the men at the top. It must be the hope of the free world and of the subjects of the communist tyrannies that he will before long recognize that to achieve the desired development of his country he will have to release the straitjacket binding the spirit and talent of its people and let them contribute the vast potential of individual effort which is now bottled up. We must expect, if and when that time comes, that the energies of a Christendom now suppressed within the vast confines of the Soviet Union will then burst forth perhaps with a zest and freshness that will be an education and an inspiration to the staider churches of the West.

It is to me ironic that the Pope so often seems like Mr Gorbachov – wanting change, but fearful of the consequences if his actions risk being deemed to undermine papal authority or the authority of the Vatican establishment. O that he would see that in Evolution God had shown that He is working His creative purposes out through a process of adaptation and that His Son's mystical body must be expected to develop in the same way!

1988 — A Year of Crisis

But the church establishment which in 1988 will be under the brightest spotlight promises to be the Anglican during the Lambeth Conference. The signs are that the Anglican bishops will spend much time on political and economic issues, cheerfully pontificate on both, and highlight both in their final communique. They will not be able to avoid the delicate and to some of them distasteful subjects of women and sex and will try to avoid creating rifts on either subject between the national hierarchies. They will probably lack time or inclination to discuss such subjects as the relevancy of the Anglican church's language and theology and its need to adapt to the changing circumstance of our times. They will almost certainly jib at speculating about the future and the new thinking that it will bring. It is doubtful too whether they will publish in advance discussion papers to enable the laity outside to contribute to their debate.

The subjects of women and sex in the context of Christ's mystical body are both complicated and it is not my intention to deal with them now save in relation to my hypothesis about Evolution. In that context I can see nothing that would lead me to believe that God has set His face either against women priests or married priests. On the latter issue the Roman Catholic church seems particularly unreasonable. So far as we know the primitive Christian church had married priests and at least some of the twelve apostles were married. The celibate priesthood was a later development brought about by later circumstances. The Roman church is short of ordinands and has already modified its rules to allow married Anglican priests who convert to Roman catholicism to remain priests. If the lack of ordinands grows worse and threatens the effective care and expansion of the Roman flock, it seems hard to believe that its establishment will still set its face against married priests or even the ordination of women. Outside Britain in the Anglican church women have already been ordained as the church has adapted to the circumstances of societies where women are recognized as having equal rights as males. They have secured those rights only as a result of struggle; and looking back on those fights and the opposition which, for example, men in Britain raised to votes for women, perhaps we men should hang our heads in shame over the way in which we defended what we narrowly and (as it proved) wrongly saw as our interests. Let us hope that at their Conference the bishops plunge boldly for adaptation and that those who object will comfort themselves with Gamaliel's advice and the knowledge that, if the ordination of women is not God's will, God will ensure that circumstances will again force change.

When I look at the issue of sex in the context of the lessons of Evolution, I sense that popular attitudes are particularly out of tune with the lessons of Christ and Evolution. We live in an age which, perhaps more than most, has put sex and sensual pleasure on a pedestal and idolised them. The propaganda of the media and advertisers concentrates on massaging the lusts of the flesh and the spiritual vices of pride and envy, and our entire culture seems to be centred on the gratification of the senses. History is full of awful warnings about what happens to societies which fall into that trap; and the Christian church has a duty to warn against it. Christ seems unequivocal in talking about the conflict between the demands of the spirit and of the flesh; and, according to John's gospel, He made it clear that the spirit's needs were prayer (communication with God) and action in accordance with God's will, with love (neither lust nor self-love) as the motivating factor. Steeped in Jewish law, He was also unequivocal in stating that marriage should be between male and female and be for life. Though there have in some societies been circumstances, and there may in future be circumstances, which in the context of my hypothesis might be held to justify polygamy, I can see none that would justify homosexual genital relations: they can never be procreative, and of their nature anal and oral sex are acts solely of sensuality. However much I sympathise with those who cannot enter into heterosexual marriage, I do not see how Christ can be squared with those who seek to put copulation between people of the same sex, however faithful they may be to each other, on a par with heterosexual marriage. I earnestly hope that the Anglican bishops will not equivocate on this issue.

But there is another reason why, I suggest, they should not do so. In 1988 the world is threatened with a new plague. No one knows yet whether like the plagues of medieval times, it will decimate the population or whether modern medical science will stop it in its tracks. In Africa AIDS has already reached plague dimensions, millions are infected with the virus and men, women and babies are dying in their thousands. Because they often die of other diseases and governments do not want to admit to AIDS, many of these deaths are not attributed to AIDS; and the AIDS danger is underestimated. In Africa AIDS strikes men and women indiscriminately; in Europe and America the disease has hitherto been mainly restricted to homosexuals, drug addicts, haemophiliacs and others infected through blood transfusions. In medieval times panic-stricken populations often branded the victims of the plague as sinners struck down by God's wrath and treated them as dangerous outcasts. In some areas of the West attempts have been made to whip up animosity of the same sort against homosexual victims. 1988 provides therefore a tremendous opportunity for Christian leaders both to reassert those Christian ideals of sexual conduct and of marriage which, if adhered to, would greatly reduce the spread of AIDS, and also to call for and support action by the Christian community to combat the suffering caused by it.

There is a further reason why the Christian churches need to review their activities to combat suffering. With the rise of public health and welfare schemes at the end of the nineteenth century a century began in which society

and the churches have looked to governments to provide
health care and other social services which had previously
been provided, if at all, mainly by charitable institutions.
It is now clear that government bureaucracies are by their
nature unable adequately to provide all these services and
that governments cannot obtain the resources to supply
the insatiable demands of their population. (Taxation
above certain levels has already proved self-defeating).
On an increasing scale charities are trying to fill the gap;
and voluntary movements, such as, for example,
Neighbourhood Watch in the field of security, are taking
off. Both in war-time and at times of local disaster it is
noteworthy how voluntary collective action promotes
fellowship and improves local moral.

Here I believe the Christian churches are being offered
an opportunity for adaptation which could much increase
their evangelisation and mission at grass-roots level. On
the analogy of Neighbourhood Watch, it should be
possible to set up Christian Neighbourhood Groups,
comprising Christians of all denominations to work
together to combat suffering in their locality and try
through voluntary service to fill some of the gaps left by
the government's social services. If members of such
groups could be encouraged privately and personally to
reflect prayerfully every day on Christ's personality as
revealed in the New Testament and the lives of some of
the "saints" they would in practice be enjoying the
spiritual food and drink deemed essential by Christ. In

this way each Neighbourhood Group would have hope of becoming a centre of Christian infection and would through the personality of Christ and the inspiration of the Holy Spirit help give a new strength and vitality to Christ's mystical body.

I found that in Whitehall, if my department wanted a committee to do or decide something, the best course of action was to table a draft. Even if it was not adopted, it did at least tend to direct the discussion along helpful lines. Papers are already flowing into Lambeth. I am not a bishop; nor was Martin Luther. I cannot claim to be a twentieth century Luther. Nevertheless I should like to end by setting out the draft which I metaphorically now nail to the massive gate of Lambeth Palace. In Christ's name I demand that the bishops wake up and consider it.

Draft Declaration by Anglican Bishops

WHEREAS we believe that
(1) God exists, supreme and personal, Who is our Creator and Who sent His Son, Jesus Christ to reveal Him to us in the highest terms capable of being understood by the human intellect – in a perfectly lived human life
(2) Jesus was crucified, rose again and lives on in those who accept Him and are infected by His

personality and inspired by the Holy Spirit and who comprise His mystical body

(3) Such evidence as we have in the Bible, in the reports of His early followers and in the examples of those people who have appeared most infected by Him and inspired by the Holy Spirit suggests that He revealed God as a God of Love; saw the goal of human endeavour as a state of personal unity and harmony with God; and taught that there is an innate conflict between the spiritual and material elements of which people are composed, that the human spirit is nourished by communion with God and by action in accordance with God's will and that these activities are as essential to the spirit as liquid and food are to the body

(4) Evolution, however it may ultimately be shown to work, is God's mysterious process for the generation of human personality at one with His and our thinking in our time-bound physical state has to be set in an evolutionary context; and

(5) As Evolution apparently works by a process of adaptation, in its physical aspects Christ's mystical body is subject to the same process

RECOGNISING that
(1) Everyone falls short of the yardstick of human conduct set by Jesus, and that much pain and

suffering are caused by this
(2) Apart from suffering caused by human failings God's creative process involves much pain and grief; the reasons for this are largely hidden from us and are probably beyond human comprehension
(3) Jesus's message of love is that individuals should use their own suffering as a means to further their harmonisation with God and should do their best to alleviate the suffering of others and as far as possible to remove its causes
(4) Jesus stressed that pride is a human failing which separates people both from God and their fellow people and that we must avoid measuring the conduct of others against our own and individually not seek to judge them
(5) Our sole hope of attaining that harmony with God for which we have been designed lies in our acceptance of Jesus and the Holy Spirit

AND NOTING that
(1) procreation through the sexual act is the means whereby the human race is continued
(2) the union of male and female in marriage has, like the life of the individual, both spiritual and physical aspects and is designed to be in harmony with God's creative purposes; yet, because of individuals' failings, it falls short of God's

intention
(3) friendship is potentially a creative element in society, a fruitful result of individuals' loving each other as themselves and a means whereby individuals help each other to become increasingly infected with God's love through Christ and the Holy Spirit

WE AFFIRM our belief in
(1) the sanctity of marriage and the need of Christian married couples to strive for harmony with God through their harmony with each other
(2) the value of human friendship as a means of mutual enrichment through the infection of Christ's personality, the inspiration of the Holy Spirit and the outpouring of individuals' personality and love

WE DECLARE that
(1) Christians need first to open themselves to the love of God and to strive to become so infected by the personality of Christ and so inspired by the Holy Spirit that their will may become in tune with God's will and their actions in harmony with His creative purposes
(2) Christians need to recognise the conflict between the demands of the spirit and the demands of the flesh – between spirituality and sensuality – and

should therefore strive not to let the gratification of their sensual appetites dominate their lives at the expense of their spiritual capabilities

(3) The Christian ideal of marriage is a lifelong monogamous union between a man and a woman united both in their love for each other and their love of God and of their neighbours

(4) Any sexual act between individuals outside marriage represents a predominantly sensual act and a spiritually-weakening falling short of the standard of conduct which a life in harmony with God demands: Christians should therefore set their sights on that standard while recognising that without the aid of Christ and the Holy Spirit they will have no hope of reaching it

(5) The state of Christian marriage is not open to everyone either because of an imbalance in the number of males and females available, some physical infirmity, some innate sexual tendency or an individual's sense of special vocation

(6) For those to whom the state of marriage is not open the satisfaction of their sexual appetite is a sensual gratification without the spiritual nourishment that comes from action in accordance with God's creative purposes and thus leads to a weakening of the grasp on them of Christ and the Holy Spirit

(7) An individual's physical self-sacrifice of chastity

out of love of God is a source of much spiritual strength
(8) Promiscuity in sexual relations is particularly dangerous to both body and spirit; physically it spreads such fatal diseases as AIDS and spiritually it is a self-centred injection of sensuality which inoculates against Christ and the Holy Spirit

And in the face of the particular danger from AIDS which now threatens the human race

WE NOW URGE all Christians to
(1) make a special effort to open themselves to the inpouring of the personality of Christ and the love of the Holy Spirit, seeing in Christ and the Holy Spirit the means of becoming in harmony with God; and
(2) strive within their own neighbourhoods to alleviate the suffering of others

AND WE CALL UPON all the churches of the Anglican Communion to cooperate with all other Christian churches in setting up Christian support groups where these do not already exist, to help the sick and the suffering and their dependants in their neighbourhoods and, wherever possible, to remove the causes of pain and grief in their midst

AND WE COMMEND for use by all Christians and

particularly all Christian support groups the following prayer:

> "Dearest Father in Heaven, we bow before You in love and awe; and we thank You for giving us Your Son to reveal You to us and to provide the means whereby we may live in harmony with Your creative purposes. May we be so infected by His personality and so inspired by Your Holy Spirit that our will may be Your will and our actions may always be inspired by Your love."

Form A   Date ....

To John Ford
20 Guildown Road
Guildford
Surrey GU2 5EN

I am interested in setting up or joining a Christian Support Group and should probably wish to acquire meditations by yourself and others on Christ as evidenced in the New Testament and the lives of Christian saints, when these are available.

Signed...
Address...
....(Street and number)
....(Town)
....(County)
....(Post Code)

Form B   Date ....

To The Rt Rev the Bishop of...............................

My dear Bishop
I am a Christian in your diocese writing to urge you to push at the Lambeth Conference for the issue of a Declaration of Belief and a Call to Action on the lines proposed by John Ford in his "Honest to Christ".

signed..
address..................................(Street and number)
....(Town)
....(County)
....(Post Code)

SOME RECENT CHURCHMAN TITLES

THE MAN WHO CONQUERED THE WORLD
GERALD BARTON
Canon Emeritus of Chester Cathedral
A powerful work of Incarnational Theology.

ISBN 1 85093 065 1 £2.95

AN ETHIOPIAN HARVEST
IVY PEARCE
Miss Pearce lived and worked in Ethiopia for many years as nurse, missionary and teacher. Her impressions are vivid and cover the nation's religion, politics, history, culture and customs.

ISBN 1 85093 072 4 £3.95

FINDING COMMUNION
J. H. CHURCHILL
The former Dean of Carlisle's wise reflections on changes in the Eucharistic Liturgy.

ISBN 1 85093 076 7 £2.95

THE LAW AND THE LAWLESS
RONALD BARTLE
The author is a Stipendiary Magistrate at Bow Street – and a Christian. He interprets his work in the light of his faith.

ISBN 1 85093 069 4 £3.95

THE SERVICES OF WORSHIP IN THE ENGLISH PARISH CHURCH
ARTHUR J. DOBB
Honorary Canon of Manchester Cathedral
and Registrar of the Guild of Church Musicians

'I feel quite sure your book will help many church people to understand better and appreciate more deeply the various features, both ancient and modern, of Anglican worship.'

– The Archbishop of Canterbury

ISBN 1 85093 073 2 £10.95

CHURCHMAN'S AFRICAN LIBRARY

Books by experts on different aspects of the situation in Africa

THE FIERCEST FIGHT
The Documented Truth About Apartheid
EARL DENMAN

'A stirring, thought provoking read.'
– *The Western Morning News*

ISBN 1 85093 012 0 £6.95

AFRICA – MY SURGERY
LEADER STIRLING

Dr Stirling went out to Africa as a UMCA Missionary in 1935 intending to serve a few years; he is still there and indeed finished up as Minister of Health in what is now Tanzania. A thrilling story by a man of vision, dedication and a character moulded by a passionate belief in the truth of the Christian Gospel.

ISBN 1 85093 061 9 £4.95

WE WENT TO AFRICA
An English Educationist in Zambia
JAMES HADFIELD

Dr. Hadfield spent ten years in Northern Rhodesia, now Zambia. He records his impressions with great honesty and tells us things we cannot discover from fleeting comments on television.

ISBN 1 85093 068 6 £4.95

ANGELS UNAWARES
PAUL BURROUGH

The author was Bishop of Mashonaland from 1968 to 1981 and was earlier Chaplain to 'Overseas Peoples' in Birmingham under Bishop Leonard Wilson. His new book is concerned with some great questions: the integrity of Christian Mission, the real issues of racial differences, the exploitation of innocent peoples, especially the young, and the true nature of Independence. Written with authority and candour.

ISBN 1 85093 095 3 £4.95

CHURCHMAN PUBLISHING LIMITED
117 Broomfield Avenue, Worthing, West Sussex
and at Warner House, Wear Bay Road, Folkestone, Kent

5983-C26
5-21